D0944261

A SURRENDER TO THE MOON

The International Library of Poetry

Howard Ely, Editor

A Surrender to the Moon

Proudly manufactured in the United States of America by
Watermark Press
One Poetry Plaza
Owings Mills, MD 21117

FOREWORD

Throughout life, we store information collected from experiences and try in some way to make sense of it. When we are not able to fully understand the things that occur in our lives, we often externalize the information. By doing this, we are afforded a different perspective, thus allowing us to think more clearly about difficult or perplexing events and emotions. Art is one of the ways in which people choose to externalize their thoughts.

Within the arts, modes of expression differ, but poetry is a very powerful tool by which people can share sometimes confusing, sometimes perfectly clear concepts and feelings with others. Intentions can run the gamut as well: The artists may simply want to share something that has touched their lives in some way, or they may want to get help to allay anxiety or uncertainty. The poetry within *A Surrender to the Moon* is from every point on the spectrum: every topic, every intention, every event or emotion imaginable. Some poems will speak to certain readers more than others, but it is always important to keep in mind that each verse is the voice of a poet, of a mind that needs to make sense of this world, of a heart that feels the effects of every moment in this life, and perhaps of a memory that is striving to surface. Nonetheless, recalling our yesterdays gives birth to our many forms of expression.

The International Library of Poetry

Artist's Profile
Eric Lee
Sacramento, California, USA

I just wanted to express how hurt we can feel when things don't turn out how we expect. A broken heart can feel like the worst thing in the world, especially when you're young. I thank God for being by my side, always.

Just Once More

All of the physical pain is nothing, and so very comforting
I'll take it in and make it all that I feel
For you the one whom I would give up everything
Do anything just to have your love revealed
Unveiled, unshrouded from my mind and the rest of my heart
It's been apparent, I'm transparent to your eyes
I only really care about the fact that we're apart
That other stuff doesn't matter, without you I would die
I know that it'll be hard, just to give me and us another chance
I can't make you the promise that it will be a perfect romance
I won't ask anything of you because I don't have much to offer
Just remember all the times and how happy we both were

Eric Lee

Rain-Song Drummer

In early summer,
I listened for the rain-song drummer
To ease the thirsty, drying plain,
To keep it thriving green and strong.
But no rain and no song.

Late that summer,
I longed to hear the rain-song drummer.
I heard the dying land complain;
The days were hot and much too long
With no rain and no song.

In early fall,
I heard the hungry cattle bawl,
And dust storms swept the grassless plain,
A once-rich land no longer strong.
Still no rain and no song.

Late that fall,
The rain-song drummer made his call,
But not a farmer could remain.
The drummer stayed away too long
With his rain and his song.

Edward V. Johnson

Our Son Came Home Today

Our son came home today
to the towering pines
and the whispering waters.
Our son came home today
in a flag-draped coffin.
We marched in the parade
along the streets festooned
with yellow ribbons.
The rifles saluted him
with a twenty-one gun salute.
The bagpipes played
and we sang to his glory
at nineteen.
His box was lowered
into the cold, dark earth
among the towering pines,
and we said, "Goodbye, soldier!"
And the waters whispered,
"Farewell, farewell, soldier."

Irma Ray Garbarino

The Question

A puff of smoke fades away
A dandelion head
Floats to oblivion
A firefly blinks in the night

Far out in the blackness of space
A meteorite crashes
Into an unknown world
Grinding to a tumultuous halt
Under the darkness of the ocean
Life shimmers

What am I?
A puff of smoke
A dandelion head
A fleeting light
That shimmers for one moment
Then darkness
A nothing
That no one remembers
Or ever even saw
What am I?

Jean Kircher

The Immigrants

The burning sun shrivels up my father's face
as he thanklessly tills the parched land.
He cannot nourish our arid bodies, minds, and souls,
another fruitless year of trying to pacify the unappeasable gods.
Will that boat with billowing sails carry us to a New World?
Afraid to hope, we scramble aboard with our
unfruitful lives tied on our backs,
precious rags that have witnessed the turmoil;
the relentless heartache . . .
days of being tossed in a cup held by a shaking hand,
nights of praying for the stilling of
the crashing, monster waves.
Then it appears. Another barren land greets us.
The cycle of tilling the soil begins as
the sun scorches father's face.
Can it be?
Rains cascade down and feed our parched souls.
New life appears. We are reborn.

Krishna Mukerji

Winter Tree Finger Painting

In freelance fashion, winter tree,
you cast your offering to the sunrise.
No adornment, self-sustained beauty,
you etch your silhouette against the skies.
Throughout the day . . . hospitality,
host . . . congenial bird bearer,
excluding no nationality.
Vagrant snowflake, rainy wayfarer,
our evening tree-clasp is of gentle yield
to the evening sunset amber light.
Finger painting poignant shadows upon lake and field,
you bough and bid your sweet good night.

Winifred L. Gonyea

Glass Houses

A sugar bowl is only full
of sweetness
so long as it is filled
with sugar.
Fill it with salt
suddenly
it develops
the deceptiveness of people
who must be sampled frequently
before we have any idea
of who or what
they really are.
To presuppose
what love should be
is to build a fishbowl
around our lives,
and even the largest aquariums
are awfully small
once we have seen, smelled, or dreamt
of the sea.

Beecher B. Brown Jr.

Icicles, Droplets of Destiny

Drop by drop,
Gutta per gutta,
"One after another,"
Or in Latin, "seriatim."
Slowly but surely,
Water freezes into stalactites, like strands
To form ice, to congeal or coagulate,
Which makes each icicle solid.
As in nature,
So in us.
The same occurs when,
Droplet by droplet,
We repeat a thought, a habit, a custom,
An act, an attitude, a trait, a characteristic,
Which helps to produce our individual character,
Our stamp of identity.
We must be ever
Vigilant as to how we
Allow these droplets of destiny
To be patterned within us.

Robert Boyce

Silhouettes

While figures on the lampshade are casting silhouettes,
A gypsy girl with spangles goes dancing on the wall,
And I can hear the music of her grasping castanet,
While figures on the lampshade are casting silhouettes.
She stamps her foot, then gracefully imposes pirouettes.
Her flashing smile escapes the flying shadow of her shawl.
While figures on the lampshade are casting silhouettes,
A gypsy girl with spangles goes dancing on the wall.

Arthur Luchan

The Catch

Throw them back, the squiggling fishes,
bursting above currents, braving the wind,
unprovoked, uninvited. Give me the pike,
the slippery trout, the crafty catfish.
Ignore the beauty, set aside the ease.
This isn't how it's done. I crave
the stretched and broken lines,
the bending poles, the reeling scars,
the gripping blisters. Give me
unbalanced struggles in rickety boats.
And what about bait? Slippery lures,
piercing trickery. Where is the fun
in a catch uncaught? Run from me, swim, fly,
try to escape. Let me hunt through icy waters,
make use of my skills. Make me earn my prize.
Let me be the savage beast
with snarling teeth, pointed mind.

Jeffrey D. Martinson

Untitled

Like a diminutive lord
of the savannah,
you stare back at me
from beneath my bed
where you crouch
on your prey, my left shoe.

You defend your prize
while I evade
your prickly claws
as I extract it from under your
fuzzy tail, yet you maul the shoe's tongue.

From your den,
past the bedspread's
dangling fringe, I drag you.
Ferociously, you cling
to the heel.

Finally, I shake you loose,
and you jump upon the bed
where you smooth your coiffure
before you hold court.

Norma Van Brunt

"La Casa Bianca"

It's barely visible from the winding, sea-shelled road.
Weeping willows, tall and tired, tenderly screening it,
Not until I turn the corner
Does the century-old clapboard emerge,
Breathing and vibrant.
In solitude, though not alone,
A trysting place for God and me,
It's ready with welcome
As it welcomed the old whaling captain
Returning from cruel voyages.
Familiar faces gone,
Their echoes swelling, pushing against the waves.
Fragrances of white lilacs midst flowering companions
Blend with salty breezes to greet me.
Ivy now past the second floor
Communicates with the widow's walk,
Gulls circling high. Free!
Many have wanted to buy the old Cape Codder.
It's not for sale,
For what price do you put on energies
And passions let loose?
Like the immortal sea,
It asks only for a heart-to-heart.

Anna Paige

Why Didn't You Call?

I shared your constant cancerous pain,
But you did not call with the awful news.
Inside my head was a recurring refrain;
It was not just a case of the blues.
My tired heart hurt, knowing not why,
Your senseless suffering far greater than mine.
Last fall, I heard your cancerous cry:
Success secured straight in a line.
God held you fast as I watched you die.
Poet, scholar, mother, so many gifts
To the world so bravely you said no blame.
On the wings of a deceased son, your spirit lifts,
May this meager verse add to your fame.
I now understand why you could not tell
That you were leaving your earthly hell.

Anne Faynberg

The Cracked Dinner Plate

The cracked dinner plate made spaghetti special;
She used it on Wednesday
Nights when
She went to her club meeting.

A hand-painted rose and its shadow
Didn't look real
With alternating buds and roses
Dancing around the rim.

She put the crack at nine on the clock-face,
Tilting the rose,
As if that was where the crack was meant.
Accepted with a twinge,

Like her mind when she looked at the rose;
It could detach and float
Up and away, out the window
Till separated from the crack.

Marie Klassen

The China Distance

Weep not for me.
Angels have lingered within my tears.
Hold not a vigil.
I have lit candles to encircle the moon.
A dress sewn with delicate thread is mine.
Woven of silk, perhaps it belongs to China.
I have travelled continents on bare feet,
Sprigs of red berries in my black hair.
There you stand unsure what language I speak.
All the while you do understand.

Travel not over seas for me.
I can make my way.
Only leave a door open for me.
You will hear my brass keys jingle.
Perhaps they joined within locks of doors
The continent of China.
I have lit candles to show me the way.
Here, there it is only a question of distances crossed.
I was born with the moon encircling me.
The angels have lingered a lifetime for me.
I believe you once glimpsed me in China.
The silk is real enough.

Hilary Jepsky

Like This Together

Wind and rocks,
We sit parked by the Waleash River,
Silence between our teeth.
Birds scattered across the sky,
Heard some Canadian geese fly by;
I know you love them so.

A year, ten years from now,
I'll remember this, sitting here
Looking at the birds in a glass sphere,
Only that we're here like this together.

We have, as they say, certain things in common.
Because of you I notice the taste of water,
A luxury I might otherwise have missed.

Blind power from our roots
What else to do
But hold fast to the one thing we know?
Let's grip the earth and let the passion burn
Like this together.

Thaddeus Jones

a warm moment in time

i loved her although she wasn't
the cutest girl in the neighborhood
couldn't afford to wear the latest threads
place her delicate feet inside the latest platforms
or shape her afro into the perfect angela davis sphere

i loved her because when she slow-dragged with me
i lost all of my insecurities and inhibitions
for the length of the 45 on the turntable

words lost their weight
while i held her tightly in rhythm her warm even breathing
caressing the side of my neck
her fingers sinfully lost inside the deepest part of my afro

when the three minutes were over
i returned to the end of the sofa and waited patiently
while others took their turns
losing themselves with her
in their own warm moments in time

Michael Harris

The Psychiatrist's Chair

With pen and paper in hand
I step up to the psychiatrist's chair
Which is my own
When I write down my thoughts on paper
Here alone in absolute silence
The comfortable reassuring voice asking
Me questions
Is in fact myself
I was not forced or told to come here
I come here alone
For my own sanity
No one cares if I come here or not
And no one notices when I leave
From this insignificant chair
In this lonely place
Only secretly I am surprised to find
Even completely alone there are still some things
I am hesitant to let myself know

Lisa Decker

Sheltered

A group of young girls gathered in a tight circle
of perfume and idle chatter.
They painted their lips with profound simplicity
and engaged in conversations of immortal innocence.
Not one knew of a world beyond their sheltered two-story house
with the Spanish tile kitchen floor and one-sided mirrors;
a world without two smiling parents, in love with each other,
in love with life.
One girl talked of saving the rain forests,
another of having ten kids and goldfish.
When are these aspirations lost?
When does one forge ahead through the fields of youth,
and arrive at adolescence, a bare age,
bereft of passion and hope?
One child, lacking the fiery blush of youth,
steps out of the circle and walks away.
The others sip hot cocoa and
speak of rose-colored dreams,
turning their cheeks to the girl who grew up
too fast.

Allison Rogers

Artist's Profile
Carole Johnson
Los Angeles, CA, USA

A few years ago, I found out I had a large cancerous tumor in my throat, which needed two operations and extensive radiation. I wrote my poem, "Listen Carefully," after a holiday occasion when all my family got together for a special dinner. My family, knowing about my predicament, did not know how to act, and I found out interestingly enough that neither did I. With just the simple showing of love and support, only a few words about the situation sufficed. My poems have been published in eighteen anthologies. I am presently writing short stories, more poems, a novel for the future, and enjoying my photography and loving husband. I am a cancer survivor, six years now, and will turn fifty in November, 2001. Poetry fell into my lap so sweetly, and easily became my sounding board.

Listen Carefully

I hate to be forced into silence
The silence hears your mental confusion
and shares your acquired feeling of waiting
to be heard from someone, anyone
You feel you can hear the humming of the batteries in the radio
not the dust falling, but the dust
ball bouncing along on the floor
competing with the spider trying to get to the corner of the room
Today, I had no intention to listen to the silence . . .
it brings out the worst in anyone
A room full of people, no one dares to say a word
stares are passed around
smiles and frowns are traded
It hurts to love your family sometimes
Why did my family go home
I guess we thought it was all necessary
to share some exaggerated frowns
or fake smiles for a while
We all wanted to share our feelings, feeling of love, maybe
but silence wins again and again

Carole Johnson

Fall

Painters dabbed their pallets with yellow and red paint
To color the leaves (especially the forest)

Under the lights 'neath the dark night
The dark, chilly night
Where worms kept themselves warm in tunnels
They dug with a voice climbing ladders higher up

That held a voice that shouted
"Uh-oh, here comes another fall"

Timothy Duffy

The Husband

Gentle hands, with love, caress the furrowed
brow of doubt, reflecting through calm and
tranquil eyes of warmth and deepest brown.

Who will touch with healing gaze, the inner
bruise of wounded heart?
His love, undaunted, soothes the inner place.
Assurance comes; sweet, comforting mantle,
where once uncertainty did abound.

Thankful is the tremulous soul that reaches
for the golden orb of priceless companionship;
God's reward to spirits joined by common grief.

How precious are the bonds that cause
belief to rest in love's soft wrap of down;
shown in tender eyes of kindness, warmth,
and deepest brown.

Carolyn Sweet Smiley

Wild Reserve

The busy bumblebee, as heavy as it seems,
is eager to draw the essence
out of summer's last thistle flower
Without knowing, it shows me its splendor;
the purple crown with its white tips
in which the brown and yellow envoy
almost drowns between the leaves of grass
in the end of ditch world, its reserve.

Even a butterfly arrives. Soon it will die.

Behind this aftermath of summer,
the wheat field has grown grayish brown,
waiting for the harvesters to come,
so dry it rustles, as if soon to burst
in self-ignition, as if warning you:
Who are you, listening so close
to change yourself, and what would you do
if nevermore this bumblebee, this butterfly,
appeared again to make it work?

Fini Lokke

Sixpence

It is the sense of time passing.
I make the program of the testament
Like the ones who burn, burn, burn

Falling on the floor,
A part of a spontaneous melody
That was hammering in my head.

It felt so surreal.
So the heart be right,
One could go up the hill of St. Lucy

Looking for an elemental place.
How many people look at themselves
In vain mirrors?

Botanical curved line, waved desert . . .
Those are all so alive.
The dew is my usual breakfast.

I do not need visionary things.
I carry all that in myself,
One copper on the tablecloth.

Yuko Ishii

Coming of Summer

Every summer, we head to the woods to isolate ourselves,
where bunnies have chewed leaves on the muted floor.
We reached the creek that flows with creamy ease
and gurgled as I tossed in an opaque stone.
The weeping willow held a refreshing scent,
its long, limp branches ripe with memories of secrets locked away
ready to be revealed once again.
Somehow it reminded me of the sunlight, bright as a scholar,
shining down on him and I until,
like an adolescent attention span,
it disappeared behind roaring clouds.
We would giggle as we ran down the trail barefoot, holding hands,
trying to outrun the sour storm rolling its way in.
And there were summers when he'd count to ten, and I'd hide
behind thick green grass past the sumac tree.
And he'd come running to my secret spot,
laughing as he chased me out into the open.
Now we place our feathery arms close around each other,
feeling the sweet passion extend in their air above us,
and we hold hands and giggle,
running off into the moonlight together.

Tracie Finley

Hornet

A honey hornet tortilla left sunning on a cracked windowsill
Collects paint chips on its backside for the owner,
Who skipped town on a sticky-handled, squeaking tricycle,
Bell ringing all the way to the school yard, following summer.
An eight-year-old's tiptoe is a slow giggle
Erupting from the creak of the old floorboards.
They have the world to tell of imperfect plans
To ignite late kitchens for the hidden cookies
They tuck in their warped, cupboard-square skirts.
The wincing chair wobbles under the weight
Of a reaching, greedy child,
Her expectant friend waiting nearby.
Unlucky, out of reach, just.
Second-best, a midnight honey drip off a buttered tortilla.
Lights off, she's coming. Lights on, she's here.
She joins us, Mother.

Spring Leherissey

In a Moment

Funny how things come and go
Events happen, this we know
They take place . . . we notice and feel
Events turn to memory treasured and behind

Fingers from the present flicker here and there
As if picking up the memories and dusting them
They are held close once and again
Embraced for a moment, then put down

From here and there memories come unbidden
Brought back by a face, a song, a scene
The mind pauses to wonder what happened
When did we lose what we had

Did we lose each other because of time or fate
Will we get back what was or do we let it completely fade
One question stays in mind . . . where are you?
These questions remain unanswered and faded

Funny how things change yet are the same
A moment here forgotten then
How a second is all it takes to bring back what was
And a moment to hold it . . . then return it to the past

Sarah Wilson

The Reason I Dance

My heels bleed, like cherry juice
Spilling from a burnt pie crust.
Drops tickle my chin before they meet
The back of my damp hand,
My brow crying hot tears of sweat,
Gluing cotton/polyester to my back.
Exasperated muscles throb in mutiny,
Yielding to movement like old taffy.
The waterfall enclosed in white ceramic
Washes away all the disease and rust,
Letting the fatigue slip off my shoulders,
Dragging it down the drain.
Snuggled neatly between the sheets
Like a baloney sandwich, sleep
Is no stranger, but finds me instantly.
Things slow down for several minutes
Before I am awakened by the next morning.
I stumble out of bed like a newborn giraffe,
And then I dance again.

Liz Pimentel

Miss You in Montana

Have you ever watched a storm
roll in across the ocean?
Perhaps the river would have to do.
He brought acrid red wine and white plastic cups.
This moment was the last as I knew him.
This was the night he intrigued me the most,
lingering on the rocks, watching
the storm roll in, waiting for him to roll out.
Montana called him tomorrow,
but I called him tonight,
away from the river and into the reach.
The field was soaked in rain and lightning,
our earnest excess of energy.
Or maybe it was the wine.
But St. Christopher had carried us there,
directly below the heavens that bellowed so wildly.
Rain kissed our skin softly, and we mimicked its tranquility.
I watched as the storm rolled in and you rolled away,
fading into nothing but these:
the letters and poems you never read.

Lauren Goldsmith

The Philosopher Stoned
For K.R.

Truth's a college man running
With a bed-sheet cape through halls
To talk of agnostics or free will
Or a comic book he's read,
Just to change his mind and do acrostics.
He seeks to bend
Reality his way by throwing it aside
For his own view of how-the-world-should-work
And just may
If his experiments ever work through.
He mixes up humors to find his Stone:
Jokes, puns, and Jedis,
And Sigmund Freud's id. He believes
In magic and Buddhist koans . . .
How in random line a form may be hid.

And when his transparency's
Fin'lly found he'll keep on running,
Though never around.

David Hirt

Bridge with My Past

I've come through life walking from where
Honey flows between trees, our wooded lot
Ambling over a split-rail, shuffling downhill,
And sneaking eight-place settings;
Myriad Sunday breakfasts,
Perking coffee, fresh juice, toast, marmalade,
Conversations stirred, pink roses, lush lilacs
There dandelion parachutes
As "wind's-shoppers" browse glen and glade
Pausing, I stately shadows cast
Hickory, maple, and oak
Where efflorescence of irises
Seasonably poke tiny heads, each long stem
Colorfully cloaked in mid-summer's dress
And my lusting sip, creasing lips, a brisk Coke,
A tale traced stacking of stone atop stone
Coursing palms, avenues, and piecing terraces
Ever skyward, plot drawn adolescence of me
Leisure reclamation . . accord of its own
Exists harmoniously . . in bridge with my past

Larry Allen Marvin

For Sister Shirl

Thirty steps up and thirty steps down,
Hopes mounting, descending
Like waves in the ocean,
Where we summered and wintered close by.
At the eighth floor landing
I prayed for your release,
At the sixth, a kaleidoscope
Of years spun me through the door:
Your guiding, your giving, our giggling.

All yesterdays are brief,
Crowded by tomorrows;
Goodbye, once a casual assuming of resuming,
Now foreshadows emptier time. . . .
Goodbye!
Goodbye!

Muriel W. Alexander

Valentine

I wish the aching
deep in my pelvis
were transformable into
red acrylic paint.
I'd dip my brush in
thick synthetic color.
I'd apply it to a
wooden box
so that every inch
was covered in crimson flames.
I wouldn't let the paint dry.
I would present it to you
immediately so the paint would
bleed on your hands.
Open the box, I'd say.
And there the heart of the matter:
Breathing. Pumping.
Dying.

Sheila Ann Regan

A Rose and a Baby Ruth

I got Dad's Super Olds 88 telling him
I had to go to the library, big paper due in history.
"Why do you need the car to go to the library, son?
It's only a couple of blocks."
"Prestige, Dad, for prestige."

Picked up Kathy out front,
we rode around town radio up, windows down
singing along with Elvis, Fats, and Ricky.

She sat real close, arm around my neck,
hand resting on my shoulder,
the prettiest girl in school.
I was wishing my buddies could see me now.

Put off and put off asking her,
afraid she would turn me down.

I remember exactly where we were
when she said yes . . .
driving across the railroad trestle
and what song was on the radio . . .
"A Rose and a Baby Ruth."

I flunked history that year.

Mike Burke

Mother Passage

Approaching me from far behind,
she opens the door at my back,
steps in through my shoulder blades,
lingers a second before exiting
through the front door between
my breast and hips where my glance follows her.

Another day it is I who enters her back door
and briefly in the ancient darkness
of her insides, makes acquaintance
with the history of my soul
before I step forward and out; thus, we walk along,
the ancient past and I,
an eternally recurring pattern of steps.

Majak Bredell

An Interview with the Artist

Beside the visitor's feet I sat, and I asked Him many things,
and as He spoke, I wrote His words of life and hope and kings.
Every image in rivers raged into pencil strokes across my page.
His words in sweet balletic grace held
sorrow and joy in one brief space.
The artist told of nectar fountains,
pomp of clouds and quivering mountains.
He talked of jewels and what He'll do
with seraph's songs and scoops of blue,
and the whispering dusk that lies between
the sky and a damsel's gown of green, and the roses'
scarlet overcoats, and trees that sway to music notes.
Every word fell quietly into miraculous calligraphy.
The artist's palette, now sacred prose,
like falling vines from porticos.
He told me murals of sun and showers, of hearts and faith
and gifts and powers, and Heaven's gates
and love and Psalms created by the artist's palms.
He spoke of tears and outspread
arms and suffered thirsting lambs.
He talked of laurel wreaths and
thorns that brought the sweetest jam.
I wrote His each inspired word, every sigh He said that day.
I asked Him when He'd come again,
and He answered, "Child, I'll stay"

Rebecca Pospical

a wish

there's a chill in the air
this warm summer night
as i sit
gazing at the stars
through a moonlit tapestry
trying to pick your face from the heavens

Shellise Lynne Piazza

Walter's Dreams

Walter in his theatre of dreams,
carefully learns his lines page by page;
waiting his turn upon the stage of nothing is what it seems.
Twisted by fears the spotlight shimmers
on yesterday's backdrops.
Old shipmates, Ginger, Fred, and Noddy
as lost and dead to him now as his useless body.
Like a temperamental friend the
cruel stroke of fate that shattered
his tomorrows stand quietly in the darkened wings.
Suddenly his heart sings. Once more
he sees things as they were.
Without a care he sails his boat across the peacock waves.
Warm breezes caress. Gentle voices beguile.
Laughing, brown-skinned girls with lips as sweet as
heather honey feather his smiles with kisses.
The curtain falls; cool hands applaud.
Twilight gleams on forgotten walls.
His performance over, Walter dreams.

Chris Senior

Ascension

South of the equator by a few degrees,
And west of busy shipping lanes between
West Africa and Rio, here the seas
Of mid-Atlantic part where there has been
A coalescence from the ocean floor of particles.
See just how they have grown
Into an island where none was before,
Now named Ascension, standing quite alone.
The ocean at this latitude holds one
Of those pelagic species never tamed,
For flying fishes playing in the sun
Disport themselves with vigor . . . aptly named.
Pectoral fins extended, they perform
So effortlessly in a graceful glide,
Above a heaving mass of water, warm
As is the air on which they safely ride.
But now, with twitching tails, they trim their glides
Into touchdown with purposeful intent.
Interrogation of the swelling tides
Tells nought of why they came or where they went.

Garth Waite

On the Approaching Death of a Friend

You will not look at yellow daffodils next spring,
Nor deep-inhale the hawthorne-blossomed air,
Nor see resplendent beauty that summer's rose can bring,
Deep-coloured blooms to make yourself aware!

You will not see again that sky of azure blue,
Nor here below, hear the hovering skylark's twittering tune,
Nor touch with feeling fingers, as you used to do,
The varied weaves produced on nature's seasonal loom!

You will not marvel at the fully-ripened fruit,
Nor pick the same from a laden-autumn's bough,
Nor will you plant the seed, or heavy-pregnant root,
To bring alive again next year the loveliness of now!

But you will surely hear the silence that is now unheard,
And you will feel the certain grip of winter's awful hand,
When your unseeing eyes that saw the former leaf and bird,
Are touched by silent sightlessness which now is planned!

Bill Guy

An Invitation

Come! Fish in the pools of my verbiage
Where the waters never run clear;
Ledge your line low for an answer
Unless you're a prophet or seer.

You'll go through waters uncharted,
Infested with snarls and with snags,
And trawl with an infinite patience,
But you'll find that my fish have no tags.

They are stunningly fast, like meteors,
But their colours are dismally gray,
And if by sheer luck you should catch one
Consume it without further delay.

If you don't, I'm afraid that its odour
Will irreverently get up your nose,
And you'll find it the same, whatever you catch,
Little matter if it's verse or it's prose.

Thomas Reynolds

Just a Thought

What do we do with the time that we save
As we hurry from pillar to post?
Do we pause to remember the source of our strength,
Give a thought to the Lord God of hosts?

The car and the plane help us travel so fast
Is the time that we save, well spent?
Do we ponder a while and give thanks to the Lord
For the brains given those who invent?

In days long ago with life a bit slow,
We had time to consider such things;
The clouds in the sky, the stars way up high,
The changes which each season brings.

With life getting faster, who is the master,
Is pleasure and wealth our chief aim?
At the end of the day, when God has His way,
Will peace be the ultimate gain?

Jean Phipps

My Mother's Washing Day, 1938

Mom would gather all her washing
This was her busy day
Five families shared the washhouse
Monday was her day
She would light the washhouse fire
With the boiler on the top when
The water started boiling, Mom began to wash
She would start with the white
Ones she liked to see them glow
So she raised them with a blue bag
And they looked as white as snow
They were put through her large
Mangle she could adjust to any
Size dropped in her washing basket
And hung on the village green to dry
Sometimes when the weather was
Looking gloomy I often heard
Her say the slates on the
Housetops are drying so there's
Hope for my washing today

Marjorie Hubbuck

A Guest in Egypt

Egypt's moon shines drunken cups of tonight,
shaking her triple bowl through haze.
The wine's sharp fires have seared my tongue,
and glutted food has sickened my taste.
The eunuch stands beside the jewelled door
that sways its panels over golden plates,
and slave girls bear the silver dish of fruit;
they come in mist-like, waving fans
in double forms of grace.
The hour has chided dreams,
and what my Eros seeks
bends like the reeds to Cleopatra's wish,
where love reflects her thousand mirrored forms
in shapes of beauty from the brazen walls.
White arms like roots lift up their hands
to draw me downward to the fecund marsh.
My mind's pool swirls its vortex of desire;
a brilliant sheen, it twists around her eye,
coiling toward her gently moving bed.

Ian MacLennan

The Photograph

I came across the photo yesterday afternoon.
My father, half the age I am now,
Stands behind my own five-year-old image,
His strong hands resting on my shoulders.
We both squint into the sun
Blazing behind my mother as she snaps the shutter.

Even in black and white,
I can smell the summer herbs in the field behind us,
Hear the birdcalls overhead
And the drone of the machinery just out of view.

I had not realized until after my father's death
Just how much I am his daughter,
How much of the old farmer
Flows in my blood
Despite my mother's attempts to civilize me.
Like him, I am nature's child.

This photo takes its honored place
On the windowsill.

Diane Crawford

Nocturnal Vigil

Indeed Plato is dead among the followers
Who rave in wisdom to destroy shadow
And await applause for deed of "gatherness,"
As if opposition can exceed death's grasp.
Mom's voice, once distraught, unloosens "wish"
From the mind's convolutions, now godless,
Woven into "thereafters" and destination,
Until asymmetry is removed from taken love.
Pauline vision fails to benumb my heart
And change the effective rhythm of passage,
The scattered petals already decaying
Beneath voiceless feet of constant believers.
And this night watch hides more the fear
Than withdraws to selfhood (of) chaste know
Ledge, instead declassifying sidereal secrets,
Raising eyes to feel the emptiness in "morrows."
Anger side winds through "whereabouts"
Devoid of illusion or prayer, agnostic and old,
The untouched ground inattentive to answers
That reconcile desires without changing sways.

Clifford W. Wilson

friday night

lost in the thought
of the chaos at a table
where everyone looks
to everyone else
for the party to begin,
for the insecurity to leave.
she wants you,
plans to line dance her way into your heart.
her friends want you to want her,
and i am suddenly called by the rhythm
of the music in the room.
i move, though i see the pressure.
they pull at you,
but nothing works,
and i know before i am told
that you noticed me.
as i make you laugh and try to ask,
the words elude my lips . . .
for a dance, would you take a chance
but you leave when i will not say goodbye.

Jessica Tanguy

beggar king

pomegranate sherbet
flowers move the temple robes
of a priest

low over the hill
a red moon waxes
the empty road ahead

white sails . . .
a wind has also shaped
the tree

rain cloud
lammergeier calls pierce the air
shadows skitter and push

knuckles relax
the grain of the wood
enters his hands

Alan John Summers

Betrayal

With acknowledgments to Oscar Wilde

"Yet each man kills the thing he loves"
And my love, he has killed me,
And like the coward with his kiss,
He did it thoughtlessly.

The Judas kiss, the flattering word
Were the weapons that he used,
Then trait'rously, with tender looks,
My answering love abused.

The bitter tears now fall like rain,
My heart pierced with a sword
More sharp than any made by Man:
The cruel, deceiving word.

But in killing me so treacherously,
His own love thus denied,
The shadow dark lies on his own heart,
His honour too has died.

The world revolves from night to day,
Time's passage heals all pain,
But honour cannot be revived
While I can love again.

Angela Barratt

The Train

I stare at the spot where we used to stand
By the train tracks and wait for the rush
Of clanging signals and screeching whistles
And the feeling of your hand squeezing mine
Your heart rate quickening
With every car that passes
And every flash from the oncoming cars'
Headlights

I stand and wait for the next train
Listening for the distant horn
Waiting for the earth to shake and rumble
Under my feet
I jump as the first car races past
I feel the blast of cool air
Laced with the scent of oil
But this time your hand doesn't squeeze mine
And your pulse remains unaffected
Because this time
I am there
Alone

Jennifer Nicole Mayberry

To Muriel on Her 83rd Birthday

September 21! We're the same age again.
For nineteen days we'll laugh and pretend
We met in the nursery where newborns are kept
And nuzzled together e'en while we slept.

That's too far-fetched to tell to our friends,
But so is the truth 'cause none comprehends
That decisions were made in seventh grade
Leading to lifetimes of devout serenade.

Your serene, regal face stirred feelings in me
Foreign to a youth so naive and free.
A decade of poverty put them on hold;
They surfaced in college, tender, yet bold.

Sixty years of marriage and I've never said
What's filling my soul, my heart, and my head:
From seventh grade on, there was never a doubt
That I would love you 'til my life runs out.

John W. Landis

Let Me Whisper

Let me whisper with you,
restless, charming waves
made reddish by the blood of Roman martyrs,
some words
while the leaves
of hours and days and seasons
are falling,
like the brown leaves
at the sunset of an epoch.

Nothing, nothing is eternal,
neither the colours of rainbows,
nor the alluring melodious notes
of this river,
nor the caress of this twilight breeze.

Only the song of ancient heroes,
echoed by your musical murmur, Tiber,
tells of the eternal rivers
of Harmony,
where we can create again, like in a dream,
the beauty of Earth.

Fabian Montanaro

Artist's Profile
Maureen Coughlan
Charlton, United Kingdom

Most of my poems are inspired through different events in life, although "A Prayer to My Father" is somewhat different from my usual poems and is self-explanatory. I wrote it following a meaning-ful dream I had of him. I believe in the power of prayer. I enjoy gar-dening and drawing. The latter I regard as a gift inherited from my father. At present, I am drawing some of the great stars of the 1940s and '50s era. My first drawing was of a young Gregory Peck, my film idol from way back, but that's a different story!

A Prayer to My Father

I fell asleep feeling ill and troubled and dreamt of you at home.
I saw your smiling face and kindly sympathetic eyes.
Did you hear my whispered prayers for intercession
and my anguished cries?
You were standing at the back bedroom window looking
out onto the garden. I stood beside you; the room was bare.
I told you how much I suffered each day; you held a hand to
your chest and with a voice filled with sympathy and certain
knowledge answered, "Yes, I know you do."
It was uplifting to be told you knew of my anguish
and were still able to care.
When I awoke, I remembered your words clearly, as clearly as
I remember your lovely roses, but I did not see them.
I guess they did not last.
Did you visit me in a meaningful dream, bringing me comfort
and encouragement? Can our hearts and minds travel
and meet in the home of our past?

Maureen Coughlan

Working Mum

Up in the morning
As the day is dawning
Lunches, uniforms ready and made
Table for breakfast set and laid
Showers first, then dress and eat
Then to the car to take a seat
Time for school, then off to work
Computer on, on time to shirk
Invoice ready, entries done
Already another day at work is gone
Fetch the kids, sort the tea
Which of the kids and where are they to be
Brownies, Cubs, Scouts, or band
Never ending, so Dad lends a hand
Washing, ironing, cleaning
Oh, no! It's already late evening
Kids in bed
Stories read
Five minutes' peace
Now time to sleep

Susan De La Mare

In the Silence

The village church stood in blissful silence,
Prayer books neatly stacked behind the door.
Splendid windows cast a multicoloured light
Across polished pew and cold stone floor.

Hymn sheets lay scattered on the faded carpet,
Specks of dust glittered in the morning light.
Memories whispered from my childhood days
And half-forgotten dreams burned bright.

The dim vestry held no muffled voices
Only crumpled cassocks of the absent choir.
And below the shadowy, dark oak beam
The light bulb hung from ancient wire.

Unlit candles graced the tranquil altar
Where words faltered, lost in earthly care.
The secrets of my heart became a whisper
In the silence, with every deed laid bare.

Pale sunlight beckoned from the heaven sent sky
And I retraced my steps with little sound.
Daisies splashed pure whiteness upon green turf
And loved ones slept beneath the hallowed ground.

Rosamund Hudson

Precious Days

I loved the days before TV
When children sat upon my knee
And stories round the fire were told
These are the memories I hold
We used a fork when making toast
Held to the blaze our hands did roast
But now we use a pop-up one
Which isn't nearly half the fun
In summer children home from school
Used the garden for their paddling pool
They never felt the need to stray
As do the children of today
Outings to the seaside as a treat
Fish and chips made the day complete
Driving home weary and ready for bed
Sandy and sunburnt, looking quite red
Nothing was costly, yet everything was nice
For time spent together does not have a price
And so I look back on the days that were free
With that wonderful possession, my memory

Teresa Burnett

black-eyed susie

skating with slick shoes,
my train, behind, splashes giddy in the mud.
slip, stumble, claw away,
laughter like a bubble between my teeth
to reach you,
sucking salty tears from flower petals,
where your hard candy lips mangle my wedding march,
where my muddy, fingerless gloves
cradle champagne glasses
from under my hat
like wide-eyed children in dirty lace,
where your soft silence brings to tears
my honorable weeping willow,
where i sit in the mud, you lie on my skirt,
where i watch you sleep in the passionate embrace of my lilies,
where i test the sensitivity of my jaws,
where only you can make me smile.

Priscilla Thomas

On Castle Land

Tic nerve, where muscle spasm tingles rip
On steel armor spine, breath pains scream, shield up
Lance tendon tear burn, in thigh meat tendered,
Of the broken trade, and rest home yet built

Fingertips numb, soil-packed, cracked skin split
Time healed over old scars, left open,
While the wily spin paper-cut Band-Aid;
Fresh stain drop for the maid, wipe away day

On greasy driveway of chariot down
No Chevy; Dodge ran forward past dead Ford
And still, citadel abode calls color
For barren angry rot wood in the wind

Treasure faces peer in antique window,
Wavering smile warps in pane distortion,
And yet, cloudbursts cry faraway gray shades
Spattering new finger-smear heart designs

Across dandelion invasion ploy
Of distant yellow umbrella fields,
Grow sweet green blade, clover aroma mixed
On castle land and peasant-tended dirt

James Ore

Balance of Strength

At middle age, review sets in,
a dusty corner where shiny tiles have been,
and the niggling mind places
that what once was into a forged lie
back amongst the honed and possible.

Where you were no longer matters,
but what you were shines bright,
and the vagueness of slackening muscles
defines that loss, as gouges left by the eraser,
an indentation of sure prowess.

Old men watch the weather.
Young men challenge it.
Middle-aged men imagine its change
to mark the wetness of where spring grass will be,
to remember the chore of raking leaves.

To close one's eyes begins the polishing,
yet voids the impeding storm,
allowing the sound of small waves
to float that idle mind in a reverie,
a quest for the balance of strength and memory.

Morgan B. Johnson

Misery's Fire and Wisdom

The light is in love with the very moment this morning
The table is at rest as a book gently grabs its company
Suddenly she cried as the window remained broken
I never looked back as quietly for that reason
Something every night is telling me it's over
My shadow feels so cold and unable to answer
Disturbed are my thoughts
Alone are those calm and quiet Sundays
Back then she would whisper and the pain would loosen
I sleepwalk to escape the never-ending drama
The hours seem to echo and laugh at my trauma
The blankets are evil as time is no matter
I lie very still and these visions become shattered
Secrets grow up and always seem haunted
Dust is so pretty, forever it must
Lust is a story and monsters stir magic meanings
My hands are so cold . . . she must be gone
I can only guess that victory comes to the lonely culture
I hope you understand
If you're reading this, then maybe you missed its happiness

Mike Pfromm

Looking Up at the Stars

Coca-Cola on gracious ice
saltwater under the sojourning sun
Black bikinis
Skin starts to burn like a fantasy
protected from the wind by the glass

Blue and green eyes
the windows of the soul
Mexican art
thinking of a black witch
saw her soul

The ship in anchor looked like paradise
The bay was paradise like a sanctuary
a place to escape
Red bikinis
Catalina Island

Another Coca-Cola
saltwater and love
If it were different the times
really beautiful eyes
looking up at the stars

George Pettersson

The Boardwalk

Wickedly the sign swells of contemptuous vacancy,
a myriad of rooms, big yard fenced in bloody stone.
Long is the stay, short and narrow the exit,
twenty years the bargain.

"Pretty Boy" of luxurious wealth,
why the confident walk, sleep of deep beauty?
Do you not know today you marry?
Can you not see the dark of day?

Pain, hate, and death, the proprietary priests,
mandating monarchies of red, of gray walls,
rape, overdoses, murder run rampant and free.
Have you any money?

End of war cannot be, it has not begun,
there are no warriors, only lost victors.
Time is not known of,
for "time" is plentiful.

Write of habeas corpus breathes of abysmal tangencies,
thick putrid air, crimson steel of sour peanut butter.
With heavy of hand frightened eyes write a tune of cruel beauty.
Black deceit.

Curtis Stowell

Morning Van Ride

The early morning road unravels before us in
a treadmill of lightly tempered conversation.
It is still dark out, and the tires hum with
the cadence of some forgotten Greek parable,
leaving behind a rooster tail of wet sky and
lost consonants. The voices inside the van
slowly begin to rise like individual
cathedrals of wisdom. I sit quietly in the
shadow of their spires, some syllables
finding me, others teetering on the verge of
never being heard. My mind floats carelessly
in the great English sea of participle
phrases and silent quotations, waiting for
nothing in particular, and trying to wake up.
Eventually, the first word of the day drops
out of my head, and into my lap like some
wingless bird. It looks up at me, barely
legible, waiting to hear its sound.

Tye J. Tyree

Walk with Me

Come walk the lane with me, the sun is high,
and lazy clouds bedeck the summer sky.
The cornstalks stand erect and fat with grain.
They bow to unseen breezes drifting by
and hear the promise of an evening rain.

We'll walk this close together, hand in hand,
and talk and laugh and say the world is grand;
and if you accidentally brush my thigh,
you'll know that even though it was unplanned,
caresses from you teach my heart to fly.

Unseen, well hidden by the corn's green rows,
we'll shed our inhibitions and our clothes.
I'll be your Adam and you'll be my Eve.
A secret that the blackbird only knows
is once you walk in Eden, you can't leave.

Long years from now when we are far apart
you'll still be walking with me in my heart.
Our naked bodies tingle when they touch,
but I blink back the welling tears that start
because you are the girl I loved too much.

Alan Cook

Missing You

Why is it on sunny summer days I miss you most?
That I long for you to share with me a bird's sweet song,
Or pick a flower for me . . . a vibrant, lovely thing?
And both of us marvel at its beauty.
I long for you to walk with me through summer meadows
And help me over stiles and help me smile again.

I should miss you most when winter brings its chill,
When snow falls, and birds are silent in their nests;
On cold, dark November days, when nothing can be seen or heard,
But rain dripping and fog swirling.
That is when I should miss you,
But that is when I just survive.

Dorothy Dobbins

A Christmas Tear

Christmas post brought her such joys
From friends both near and far
Carols, crackers, and children with toys
Nothing could her happiness mar

This first Christmas without her
What pleasure can there be
Joyous memories of her linger
But the lights are out upon the tree

How can I face this festive season
What can I give her now
My love! But what is the reason
I cannot kiss her brow

Streamers lead only to sadness
Tinsel strands no longer glisten
Cards may bring their hope of gladness
If only to her voice I could listen

Silent is the breakfast table
Presents unopened lie forlorn
My heart would lift were I able
To see her smile this Christmas morn

Geoff Powell

Say It While You Can

The sparks no longer leap and flash,
Now I see them spent and dim.
They fade into a ghostly ash
Then dwell among the seraphim.

How many hours are wisely used
When the gift of life defeats its time?
"Three score and ten" had been abused,
When spangles glittered in its prime.

The flush of autumn begins to cool,
As I search my mind for flecks of gold
Lying dormant in a youthful fool,
While wisdom now is growing cold.

Ash to ash and dust to dust,
A million thoughts I've failed to save.
Those flecks of gold hide in the rust,
And will disappear into my grave.

So long as thoughts will flash through souls,
I hope that sparks will start a flame,
And in its aftermath among the coals,
Perhaps a verse will birth a name.

Milo Field

Artist's Profile
Gloria Gastellum Rapp
Tucson, AZ, USA

This particular poem was inspired toward the end of the year-long ill-ness of my dear friend, Megumi Shimizu. She was a valiant warrior as she reached the death of her spirit during her last three weeks of life. She retained her humor up 'till the day of her death as she visit-ed with friends and family in her hospital room. Never giving up, she finally agreed to have hospice at the end. While she was being trans-ferred to a waiting room in the hospital, the last crisis hit her body and she went into a coma. Just sitting quietly with her made the poetic floodgates open. The last thing I wrote for her was printed on the pro-gram for her memorial service. For the rest of my life, I will have so much to express about her personhood and the meaning of friendship, and especially about the joy of life she held so close and expressed through her every breath. She was my hero.

Nearing the End

A year from splendor to ending
I have watched her body curl into itself
Pain finding its way past her surface
Attributing to the cough that wells deep
So that she does not walk tall anymore
Her frail body curls in upon itself
Everything is looking small and frail now
But the cancer cannot hide her beauty
Her light shines with such brilliance
I want to reach in and pull the cancer out
But if I did that my unaccustomed hands
Would pull something beautiful instead
So I reluctantly leave the pulling
So God can work His magic
We here must let her bear her cross
We will keep loving her with our tears
Share our memories of magic
And make chicken soup until the very end
Whenever that hateful day will come

Gloria Gastellum Rapp

The Wisdom of Experience

We are never too old to learn and never too old to teach
Never too old to grow and never too old to reach
Reach out and lend a helping hand to those who are in need
Of the wisdom of experience so we may plant a seed
A seed of knowledge rich with truth, a gift with love entwined
From which a rose will blossom in God's own special time

No one can escape this life and as a child remain
With pure, untarnished innocence, without a guilty stain
The world is alluring, yet from us sin will take
Peace and joy and harmony, God-given for God's sake
He taught us what we need to know, He taught us how to live
And when one fails to follow, He taught us to forgive
He lifts us in our darkest hour from the grip of pain and strife
To become a better person, to live a better life
Such wealth we gain from our mistakes, we need not sorrow hold
Its precious ore we can refine into a pot of gold

Janis Hoover Miner

Remember the Past

My Nan remembers years filled with smiles and
with tears as she tells me her stories today.
She saw men who did cry when they said a
goodbye by their loved ones as they went far away,
away to a war which took lives by the score
and returned them to loved ones all tattered.
Some returned in a mess, a state of undress and
others would simply be scattered.
I look up at my Nan and take hold of her hand,
I see a tear fall from her eye.
I love the stories you tell, Nan, and I want to
hear more, but I really don't want you to cry.
My Nan, she's okay, and wanted to say what a
wonderful life she has had.
She's lived through a war and oh, so much more, and
then she gave birth to my dad.
We put a man on the moon and heard the best
tunes from pop stars and legends of old.
We burnt what we could when we ran out of
wood so we wouldn't go hungry and cold.

Linds Wood

A Child in the Street

Walking down a grey and narrow street
where soft rain was falling sadly,
two children walked before me,
and beauty came laughing and dried her tears.
The child that held me there, wondering,
was still only the height of a stock corn,
and yet in her slim arms
she clasped an infant sleeping soundly.
Her blue dress was all crumpled
like a windy sky, her shoes
and her small white socks
all spattered, but fit to tread the stars.
Her torn coral-coloured coat
had red hair spread upon it,
like the mane of a roan red steed
spread shining into the dawn.
She could not know the things I wished her
as she walked away along the street,
the street dark when she had left it,
and the infant sleeping in her arms.

Jean Orr

The Polmaise Pit Disaster
This poem is about a pit disaster

The Polmaise cage over wind 1934
It happened at the changeover of shifts
Both upwards and downwards cages were full of men
The men on the downward cage got it worse
As the cage hurled uncontrollable to the pit bottom

Down in the coal mines fathoms below
Risking their lives day by day they must go
A living to earn, a penny to save
Never knowing the minute it may be their grave

I will always remember, my memory is kind
The Polmaise disaster, the cage overwind
I was there that day to help those poor men
My heart bleeds for them now as it did for them then
As we carried them to the old joiner's shed
Not knowing who was living, not sure who was dead
As the ambulances hurried them away
I watched mothers crying, I saw fathers pray
The winding man, he took the blame
But the whole cover-up left the management in shame

Alexander Laird

Erosion

Time lapped at my toes
An eternal aquatic murmur
White-capped and ceaseless
Knocking over all in its path

Met at the edge by sand
Densely packed into uniformity
Sitting, waiting, for time to take its toll

Wind and rain made their assault
Time only strengthened
Its rise and fall more violent
A powerhouse of destiny

Unable to move the sand fell victim
Control was not theirs to be had
For time was unequaled
Even by the foolishly stubborn denials
Slung about by the sand

So time stormed ahead
And becoming part of the past
Henceforth only a memory
The beach forever washed away

Cary Smith

Untitled

Perky crayons singing soprano
Rejected braces taking notes
Confused flannel pjs tripping
Skeptical cacti climbing ropes

Stubborn polka dots laughing freely
Helpless paper dreaming gold
Arrogant French horns teasing skis
Outdated postcards growing old

Chartreuse ponies writing novels
Preppy freckles ending brawls
Glaring band friends sewing quilts
Charming tennis racquets taking falls

Secret footprints praying deaf
Storytellers believing that all is well
Chicken tasters seeking unhidden destinies
Only sugar and time can tell

Heather Marie Hoehn

Yalta

Daybreak over Yalta.
The Black Sea, perversely blue in lucent light,
Is more exotic than I ever thought to see.
My sleepless eyes investigate the scene.

I wonder whether this adventure,
The final twitch of an obsolete career,
Promises anything as grand
As this mysterious, fabled, aged place.

The eastern hemisphere has slipped below in darkness
And I am disconnected . . . out of time and place
Between cultures . . . one of which was mine,
But changed beyond my pliability
And one I never could possess,
Except by lineal descent and memory inherited.

My home is ancient, too, but my forefathers, manacled,
Brought alien ways to recreate the things they understood,
To chain remembrance and invent new myths.

Those myths were mine but fed a fatal hunger,
And I am here, with only vestiges of now and future,
Gazing apprehensively at Yalta.

John Hanan

A Child's Prayer on Bent Knees

Please change me from being thin and frail,
And help me to read good and fast in braille!
Thank You, Lord, for my guide dog Flo;
There's not many places we can't go.

I find it hard to feel the shine upon my shoes,
And keep picking papers up in twos.
I've never seen a rainbow or a rose!
They must be marvelous, I suppose,

And as I lift my face toward the skies,
Imaginary rainbows and roses pass my eyes.
All the world seems bright and clear
Not for me to see, but I can hear.

Keep me from all dangers, Lord, I pray
That I may help others on their way.
Thank You, Lord, for my work and my play
For this is my prayer at the end of my day.

Ken Brown

Tomorrow

I stood in summer rain, watching
the pain of my city wash away.
The town hall clock that had stopped
the day the soldiers came, groaned
back to life, chiming the wrong hour,
but we didn't care.

Flowers bloomed on cue, nodding
their heads to the breeze in approval.
Children played in once deserted streets,
their laughter tinkling like crystal.
Dogs barked, cats meowed, birds sang.

An old lady lifted the hem of her dress
and waltzed to the Strauss in her head.
Today, we won't count our dead. That
we will do tomorrow, in the awful shock
of peace.

Jerry Hughes

Love, the Magician

That night I lay with throbbing wounds.
You curled a feather arm around my neck
And kept the terrors of the night at bay.

That day I longed for night to come.
You smoothed my aching with a smile
And telescoped the long day down.

That year I roamed the whole world round
And lost my way en route.
You sailed across the seas to me
And brought me home at last.

Geoffrey Carne

A Gift for My Mother

I had no grandma, you know, I had an aunt instead,
who raised my mum and cared for her and tucked her into bed.
I thought my aunt was wonderful, so generous and so gay,
until the day I heard the tale of a far-off Christmas Day.
My mum had asked, as children do, for a pony and lots more,
and when she woke there was a note to advise her of the score.
A greedy, undeserving child who needed a hard lesson,
whose legs were very tightly bound and on her sacks of Hessian.
The tears began to tumble down, so bitter and so sad,
she couldn't understand the deed that had made her really bad.
She saw her sister's gifts, bright ribbons for her hair,
no presents would there be for her;
it was more than she could bear.
For seventy long, remembering years, she thought and prayed
to erase the suffering of that dark and painful day.
Was I really greedy then? Were they so terribly unkind?
My reply was nil, for cold fury had filled my vengeful mind.
Although my mom had known no ma, no true sister and no brother,
God's gift to me was a warm and wonderfully loving mother.
That dreadful day of darkness was a hundred years and more;
may no child ever know that cruel and hurtful score.

Glenda Joy Adams

Prisoner of War

Who can see the changes
that are hidden deep inside?
Are they just ignoring
all the words we cannot say,
covering up the damage
with the medals pinned today?

We kept our thoughts within us
for a man withholds his pain,
a pain that slowly eats him up
and clouds his thoughts each day.
Suffering in a silent world, a prisoner of war,

our families were so happy
just to have us home again.
They knew that we were different
as they held us in their arms.
Brave and noble soldiers
whose scars were tucked away,
men who'd live in silence
with the legacy of war.

Janette Hill

Artist's Profile
Anne Coghlan Charlton
Plympton, South Australia

This poem is an actual account of a sulphur-crested cockatoo that I saw in Queensland. Its ability to wildly screech "hello" terrified the flock of birds it appeared to wish to join. Amidst the typical bush sounds, the call was harsh and strange, and the cockatoo stayed isolated and alone on a broken white ghost gum branch. Suddenly and harmoniously, the cockatoo soared and not only joined with, but led and soared with the flock.

The White Cockatoo

A snow-capped canopy so richly tinted feathered gold
Gently blanketing the bush and towering eucalyptus
Yet even so, the stillness of the eerie creaking undergrowth
The creeping, clicking, crawling living bark

Is challenged, is even effaced, is now confusion
And the perfection of its complacency is questioned.
The very order of nature, its frailty, its strength, its being
Is so harshly shattered 'midst the serenity of dawn

And so a single, strongly human cry screams forth
From the distinctive isolation of a broken distant branch.
A rough, strange, distorted "Hello" screeches out harshly,
Destroying the magnificent serenity of the Australian bush.

And one isolated flash of white and yellow feathers
Terrifies and scatters the still gathering of its own kind
From which human ignorance prevents its bonding
And so emerges solitude, loneliness, and dampness of dawn.

Yet the caller senses freedom even as it cries out still
And soars to join the wild, white screeching mass
To harmonize a symphony of classic bushland tunes,
Then in turn to lead the flock
Of white sulphur-crested cockatoos.

Anne Coghlan Charlton

The Girl I Used to Know

Where is the girl I used to know?
What does she do? Where does she go?
I remember that cheeky smile and those twinkling eyes,
That strange stare and that look of surprise.

Vivacious, precocious, with energy to spare,
Laughing and playing without a care.
As bright and as clever as a girl could be,
As individual as anyone could see.

The music she played was emotion in sound,
For her musical abilities she was quite renowned.
And as the breeze danced through her long hair,
Her charismatic presence filled the air.
Bright and bubbly, she enthusiastically,
Dreamed on unrealistically of what life could be.

She faded away to someone I don't know,
She doesn't care what she does, or where she will go.
I'll just have to wait, to wait and to see,
If ever she comes back like she used to be.

Karol Antipas

The Gold and Grey of the 20th Century

On a snowy, wintry Christmas Eve
People were rushing everywhere
For it was a special night indeed.
Joy, happiness, and merriment was everywhere to be seen
But one little boy could hardly be seen.
Nobody noticed this little boy so meek and weak,
Nor his ragged clothes and bare freezing feet.
He had no family and no home for to go,
And food was but a memory from long, long ago.
He passed many a home and looked longingly at beautiful sights,
Yet this little boy lived each day in sadness and fright.
Surely, where there is so much
Happiness people will share it with me,
Said the little boy hopefully, repeatedly.
He looked into many homes, yet no one heard him knock,
And those who did looked upon him with great shock.
Many feared he may be carrying illnesses and disease
And even others said, why should we this dirty, ragged boy feed?
Everywhere, he was denied entry and pushed away hurriedly.
Consider then this sweet, poor little boy and many, many more
Who, in the twentieth century have
Time and time again been ignored.

Marie Markopoulos

The Artist

If I could paint a portrait of your eyes,
misty with tears and colour your breathy sighs
in shades of sorrow,
grey and moist and yearning for a bright tomorrow,

if I could paint a portrait of your lips
reddened with cherry wine sips,
then shade your troubled brow
with all the tenderness my touch would allow,

if I could paint the bouncing sway of your hair,
bright with golden lights and oh, so fair,
then I count myself an artist, who, in truth, dared to create
a portrait of your radiant youth and hand it in my heart.

If I could paint the glow of you
smiling by the candle's light,
the scent and feel of you, intoxicating me so,
if I could only paint, my artist's heart you'd surely know.

Oh, and this portrait hangs alone in the gallery of my devotion,
every brush stroke a heartbeat of emotion,
and a pledge to you eternally, while the moon glides above,
this enraptured soul paints you with love.

Jenny Finch

Genesis

I stain clean white
innocence
as I transcribe a
scribbled mess
of illogical thought
neatly writing
thoughtlessly copying
word
for word
for word
all that logic has created.
No mess here
even innocence has its place
within the margins
of the gentle ink bleedings
that flow effortlessly
from beneath my
fingers.
All that bleeds
will die.

Leanne Wheeler

In Paradisum

For every pain, I have a love.
So I collect pains
like disease-ridden feathers
discarded by beautiful birds of dark death
gliding in the ascension of ecstatic angels.

Through hollow eyes
I can see the all of everything
and incandescent Mary;
I can taste the smell of touching sound,
it is chocolate velvet bourbon;
I can see the beauty of dark,
a bloodied fifty dollar bill.

I can see the entire mural
in Paradisum.

Martha Buckley Sullivan

Welcome the Rain

Tonight, when the moon is full
and the trees are illuminated
by its silver light, when the
wild geese follow their instincts
south, and owls glide silently over
frozen fields, when the sound of
my laughter echoes across
the landscape (once barren and
full of despair), I will whisper
into the wind, and it will
shout my joy across the plains,
carry it eastward over rivers
and mountains, gather it together
and rain it down on you.

Roberta Sampere

Garden Spaces

It's only June, but August scorches the air.
And the ancient grace of the gingko tree,
with green fans, gallivanting about,
challenges the very air.
Fireflies hurriedly draw in the honeyed fragrance
beyond compare of the stately linden tree.
Japanese beetles lustrously and
sleepily feast on roses, endlessly.
And yet, every year, without care,
their velvet petals bloom again, gloriously.

Lavender blossoms delicately bow their heads
to the golden-coated bees,
bumbling along, near-missing butterflies on their path to nectar.
The yarrow plant with amethyst
jewels atop, softly feathers the view.
Profusely strong chamomile, bent and spreading,
sleeps now on the ground.

Touching the human spirit with elegance, lilies worked in wax
burst forth and color the landscape.
And the bonny lupine cheers the open spaces,
and the primroses show their faces.
Reflective time in the garden, listening to the earth,
and elevating the mind.

Yvonne M. Grahovac

Watersmeet at Millennium

On the bridge, I turn at the heart of it all.
Suspended over the confluence of rivers, I rock
In my mortal boat, buffeted in the blending of the flows.
What brought me here to this clever, dipping pull to center,
This gravity of the soul?
Beneficent conspiracy of the many-armed universe,
Dancing, intriguing, inviting?
The appearance of chance? The patterns of chaos?

With me may stand all humankind
In our millennia of recombinant past,
And the streams of time and consciousness and mortality meet and
Merge in us as we turn inward to face the ever-new.

Struggling to hold the wilding waters within me, to smooth their
Surging immediacy to tameness, containment.
I hear children cascading down through the woods.
Eyes shining, shouting, expectant, they erupt into view.

Yielding my place on the bridge, I will build
No tabernacle of the spirit here today.
"Move on!" the waters call out. "Journey on!" they advise.
When I look back, the path is pulsing
With pilgrims to Watersmeet.

Amanda McNeill Bandy

Artist's Profile
Ted Johnson
Charlotte, NC, USA

Simply stated, having this poem published gives me the opportunity to immortalize one of the greatest women who ever lived.

We Didn't Know

Ma worked hard scrubbing Miss Anne's floor,
and washing Miss Anne's clothes, and cooking
Miss Anne's food, and raising Miss Anne's children, too.
She got sick to her stomach every time
that Miss Anne's prissy little nine-year-old would call her girl
('cause Ma was only almost fifty),
but she would smile and say
"Yes, ma'am," 'cause that was her job,
her expected place. And we was young
and didn't really understand what Ma
went through, 'cause she didn't let on.
She just came humming "All My Trials, Lord, Soon'll Be Over."
And we couldn't understand that that song and
such others gave her strength and relief, and that believing
that the Almighty would one day
right this wrong was the only thing that kept her going;
'cause the twenty-five dollars she got a week from Mr. Joe and
Miss Anne sure didn't give her much to look forward to.
And it didn't make no difference if the weather was bad,
or if Ma's veins in her legs was hurting,
or if her back was aching from all those days before.
She pressed on anyway. 'Cause
that twenty-five dollars she got a week
from Mr. Joe and Anne sure didn't give
her much to look forward to.

Ted Johnson

Mime

He leans in and touches his lips to mine,
His face white, his lips red,
His black cap turned around;
I am kissing a mime.
I grab onto his black jacket and
Taste his white makeup.
His lips are warm,
His tongue tastes like tobacco.
Who is beneath the makeup? No matter,
I am kissing a mime.
I lean back and open my eyes.
His makeup is smudged and
I can almost see his face.
Now I wear the white makeup and
He tries in vain to rub it off.
I am kissing a mime and
We are both in disguise.

Laura Beth Kabakoff

harvest trail

by witches' chants
near graveyard's end
who lose the trail
and vanish then
in restless leaves
that taunt and tease
autumn trees
wind whirl in
lost memories
sing of ruin
as clouds dance by
a hallowed moon
never found by
light of day
by witches' chants
led astray

John Thomas Becker

Divided State of Hysteria

A ninety-something degree subtropical hell
welcomes the invasion of migrating parasites,
their buzzing overcoming the sweltering peninsula

that has submitted itself to the alien pestilence,
refusing to conform as part of the ingredients
to the melting pot now split into fragmented pieces.

Bewildered citizens surrendering to the foreign noise
pledge their allegiance to a divided nation
without the courage of the original natives

forced long ago onto reservations
potentially awaiting future occupants,
pale ghosts of a people with a lesser spirit

become the tragic chorus lamenting a bilingual anthem.
A country gazes at its fallen stars,
waning into the night like the official language

while few remembering the legacy of their forefathers
restore determined replicas of Betsy Ross,
boldly sewing the torn stripes back together.

Amanda Rose Taulbee

Blitz

Every night the bombs rained down,
Destroying buildings in London town.
Night after night explosions and fire,
Sirens wailing, conditions were dire.
People rushing to get underground
Away from the bomber's ugly sound.
Children running helter-skelter
To find the nearest air raid shelter
And refuge with their family and friends.
Raid after raid, it never ends.

Then in the cold night of day
Streets and houses blown away.
Wholesale destruction and piles of rubble.
Long dark days of wartime trouble.
Squadrons of spitfires took to the sky
To stop the German aircraft on high,
Sending them back o'er the white cliffs of Dover.
We'd won . . . the battle of Britain was over.
But had we won? What was the cost,
With so many lives and buildings lost?

Anthony Butcher

Artist's Profile
Shirley A. Honeycutt
Tallahassee, FL, USA

"As Seasons Change" came to me as I'm made aware that I'm no longer eighteen but thirty years older. Looking into my mirror, I see none of my youthfulness of my own. "As Seasons Change" helps me to put it all in order and made me see my life is not at all bad. I'm forty-eight years old, married for thirteen years and the mother of four sons and grandmother of two. A teacher's aide and artist, I love writing poetry and novels.

As Seasons Change

As seasons change and I grow older
I'm blessed with memories of days past.

As seasons changed and I grew wiser
I'm blessed to have grown older.

As the seasons change and the years come and go,
things that once seemed so important are just things
that come and go.

As seasons change and years come
I'm made more aware that life has its endings
and there's always new beginnings.

As seasons change and I've grown in years
love came, family came, and the nest is left bare.
I'm blessed to have had the straw, the sticks, the leaves,
the mate, and the love of God to build my nest upon.

As seasons change and new beginnings start, it's as if the
frozen winter earth is releasing its sleeping souls to the
warming spring sun.

As seasons change and my days are fewer my steps are shorter,
my sight is fading, my hair, once black, spoke only of youth,
now greying with wisdom.

Shirley A. Honeycutt

Touch of Butterflies

By kneeling on his fold-down bunk he could see
through the window bars and across the roofs
to the church tower.

There against a black backdrop of shower clouds,
gulls glowed white in rogue shafts of sunlight.

They wheeled and shrilled
like tormented spirits seeking an eternal rite,
and he felt a jab of fear
that he might have to face a higher court,
even though he had confessed
and had put the lies to rest.

But for now his conscience, sentry of his soul
was purged by the punishing realism
of jangling keys and slamming doors.
And there was a lifetime to rewind and replay
tantalizing flashbacks of freedom,
in fields of wind-bowed thistledown
harboring the touch of butterflies.

Brian Morgan

Some Time Ago

In Kent on a long weekend
Leaves crusted green in the paint of the sun
The detachment of pebbles and dinosaurs

The menacing calm by mid-afternoon
Of heat in the countryside
(Too obscure for a forecast of weather)

A new birth for five minutes
At the start of a summer's day

Opacity in neo-gothic spires

Gaze at that merest entity on Earth
A web of light and shade cast by trees on grass
Enticement underfoot

On a warm weekend in Kent

T. M. MacRobert

Distant Memories

Kept locked away in a corner of my thoughts,
Memories of someone I thought I loved.
I still recall the way he held my hand,
And the blissful glow he gave me.
I remember our first kiss under a starry sky,
Then later, our last goodbye.

The tears have long since been shed and yet
There is still something, a bit of passed emotion
That still creeps out occasionally,
But it's only a distant memory.

Lucy-Ann Rotherham

Airbrushed In

Sleep well tonight
beneath this "Starry Night,"
or at least if you wake tossing,
imagine me a good thing,
even in light of those dangerous things I said.

Entertain thoughts and dreams of us;
pictures of forever and fairy tales
that reach beyond the stratosphere.

Remember my voice like I remember yours
echoing in my head, phone against my ear;
all that is missing in sound quality and visuals
gets airbrushed in like Hubble pics
of far off planets and gaseous clouds.

Howard Garwood

Cold without December

She sits alone in a bone-cold room
Crisp autumn outside
Its cool fingertips pressed against the windowpane
Her blank eyes stare at the TV screen there
Its blank screen shows no emotion
But black
11:00 and her father's not home
Mom waits in the kitchen on the telephone
Forgotten the back door is open gaping
A gust of evening sweeps in
Fresh and keen against the nostrils
Suddenly the TV volume blares up
Just soft enough that some stifled sobs are
Seemingly silenced

And her mother blinks

But the breath of wild night has already
Departed

Tracey Mohr

That Relationship

There was a hand she loved to hold,
a face she loved to touch.

There was a voice she loved to hear,
a smile she loved to see.

There was a guy she said she'd never forget,
a guy she'd always love.

There was a relationship she'd put her heart in,
a relationship that changed her life.

There is a girl who is gone now,
a girl who threw her life away for that guy,
a girl who I'll never forget.

Lindsay Boettcher

Old and New

Today it's another new arrangement
of the same old inventory.
Family photos hung for strangers,
stories whispering in the corner,
pendulum clock, tongs, baskets,
ice picks, things heavy with time;
wrought-iron roses, old school desks,
no students, a park bench rimmed
with mire, without the old men or park.

Lives, stories, followed them right
into the shadows not like now;
new, clinically efficient, light
and disposable, this place,
how can it hold the stories now?
Now that it's part of the new,
cradling these things, this place,
like a colander, straining
to catch the last whisperings
from my grandmother's face.

Grant Mitchell

Melody of Spring

Today the trees are laced with miniature green leaves,
Whiffs of pear and pink apple blossoms scent the air.
The lilac wears a crown of lavender blossoms,
A gentle breeze is kissing the tulips so fair.
The old pipe wind chimes dangle from the apple tree,
Tapping out melodies directed by the wind.
A pair of squirrels race up and down the maple's trunk,
And the week's wash hangs on the clothesline, firmly pinned.
My neighbor's black dog barks loudly at the mailman,
A calico alley cat walks along the fence.
Children's voices echo along the busy streets,
Caterpillars in the elm tree are spinning tents.
Fluffy white clouds in skies of blue are playing tag,
Chasing each other as the warm wind laughs with glee.
The robins and bluebirds search for fat, juicy worms
And I, on the patio, sip a cup of tea.

Genevieve Forsythe

Franconia

Written upon visiting the Frost Place, Franconia, New Hampshire

He lived here but a short time long ago
in this white farmhouse on a grassy slope,
when he held out a rather wistful hope
of harvesting what might be willed to grow.
Instead, the fresh New Hampshire mountain breeze
brought woods and wildflowers to the farmhouse door,
where he surrendered to the Muse, no more
a farmer than the birds and deer and trees.
Today, behind a barn beside the home,
on paths where benches punctuate his love,
I try to follow in the footsteps of
the plowman who would rather write a poem.
This terra firma served some decent yields;
his cornucopia, from other fields.

Catherine Chandler

Denying Evolution

I thought I saw myself today
in a pool of sacred water, drowning.
And as I clutched desperately to life,
it occurred to me that once I had gills
swimming in a primordial sea.
This is what the esteemed scholars tell me . . . they are wrong.
I have not come from anything but dust,
and now to dust I shall return.
Buried for eternity in a sea of guilt and shame
for giving thought and reality to my dreams.
I dream of you and my soul weeps.

Natalie N. Johnson

A Whole VCE for Nothing

I remember I didn't remember who you were
till I saw you on the news,
your pretty eyes staring back at me.
Do you remember that photo being taken?
Did you hear the flash?

Did you know what was happening
when it happened?
Were you alive when you hit the ground?
Did you hear the tires screech
and the music in the background?
And did you know that the music wasn't music?
It was screaming, and it was tires.

I didn't know six months ago
that you had six months to go.
You were ticking down.
You were a bomb
and you exploded.

And I didn't remember
till I saw you on the news.

Kaitlin Van Hooft

Silent Exchange

Are you listening? You, with your head tilted,
your shoulders hunched,
a wisp of hair twisted around your finger;
or is your mind curled in on itself like a fern frond,
leaving me only your unlined face, and even that turned away?

How can I reach you? I know you reject advice.
I, too, have sat rigid, withdrawn,
resenting the flow of words
washing over my head,
holding my breath,
not to drown in unwelcome concern.

You have given me life; I must walk tall through the land.
You have given me eyes; if I stumble I'll stand again.
You have given me strength;
if I'm trapped, I'll fight my way out.
You have given me feelings, although I can't share them with you.
You have given me pride; I make the decisions, I.

Zia Atkins

Empty Passages

Brisk struts
Galloping slow drip-tumbling rubbish
Inside corners and dead-end alleyways
Transitory homes
Threatening cleanliness 'til the next gust comes
Wheezing and weeping of its own sour stench
Acting like a lobotomized seagull
Lifting up with the currents and falling
Not quite sure of who they are

William Pritchard

Climbing Parnassus

I dreamed I Mount Parnassus climbed
and there my Muses met,
and many lofty thoughts I rhymed
'mongst that poetic set.
In similes and image great
came philosophic lore
and floated from my laureled pate
profoundest metaphor.

Of things celestial did I pen,
great things of Earth as well,
and other mysteries 'yond my ken
ere that poetic spell.
But when my fancy soared too steep
in midst of wondrous rhyme,
I slid from that artistic sleep
and dreamland's mountain climb.

Yet from my pen proud verses strut
with inspiration still
though my Parnassian Mount be but
my bedtime pillow hill.

Muriel Deitch

Artist's Profile
Katrina Plumb
Bristol, United Kingdom

Choreographing calligraphy is my favourite occupation. All of the dancers are supple. As adjectives pirouette around the page, empowered by verbs to enliven the nouns, the poet is a privilege spectator. If I grow up, I should like to be a poet. In the meantime, I am working for an accountant and training to be a teacher.

Mathematics

Division came first
First to separate
Initial cloud burst
From torrents which fate
So freely dispersed

First first, then second
From second to third,
Fourth, fifth, sixth, seventh
Addition inferred
All formed a spectrum

What is the sea and
Man when combined?
Try subtracting land
And then you will find
What needs can't withstand

Go forth: Multiply!
Make parts again whole
Let loneliness die
The loveliest goal
Call all laws defy

Katrina Plumb

Zany-Striped Love

The bee is
Ministering to the flower
Growing it
Hovering over a candelabra of blossom-cups
The living altar

Emily Taussig

Copy Quick

Designer genes;
Ovum replicatus.
Uniqueness lost in the multiplication of
Brown eyes . . . here . . . and there . . . and there . . .
Living copies one of the other
An ever-expanding sea of you.

You who challenged wiser souls,
Opened doors to a more brazen world,
Unwrapped the mysteries of DNA
Repeated here, ad nauseam.

Perhaps the experiment was too bold?
Lust for fame, an
Evanescent pleasure at best,
Achingly reminds us that
Sin is not confined to murderrapegreedhateenvy . . .

Unless we see our folly, we will continue to
Raise our waxen wings too near the sun and
End in a bang and a whimper.

Janice Hudley

Immaterial
For Jack

Today I looked out on the world
and I tasted
you.

I watched this blushing, Indian-paint summer sunset
and I felt your hand go stealing over
my cheek.

When a beautiful cup of coffee filled with the kind of foam
that sailors dread emblazoned my insides,
then I remembered your arms, and how
quick they are
to wrap around me.

I drank up the night sky in the same tones of blue
that God dreams in, and while I stared, I sensed that I
was being watched, and heard your
perfect eyes close,
thinking of me.

Emily Jane Rogers

Vertical Indecision

A stairwell changes all perception
with its echoes and blank stares,
its encounters unexpected.
It is a vertical hallway of transition,
and it can reveal the true condition
of where you stand
with someone.

Can you touch that person
as you climb,
or are you just following?
Waiting for the right floor,
waiting, silent, through this change,
where things unknown might be said,
when that pretty head
you thought you knew
has become just a head
in front of you.

Robert Bell

A Little Fresh Air

Faded,
the still-grand drapes
galed outward into the wind,
flags of tumult
fleeing the long-shut gilded windows
which were thrust open
by some new hand.
The great hall heaved and exhaled
its static confinement,
awash with tides of fresh air,
letting her skirts fly,
rushing into equilibrium,
joining the weather.

Overwhelming,
precipitous,
and welcome,
the house breathed.

Heidi B. Morrell

Charley Gone Sleepwalkin' Again

Mama, Charley gone sleepwalking' again!
Chasing 'em old jack-o-lantern's tunes!
Chasing 'em old Robert Johnson's blues!

A rickety chair, a stomping down,
A clickety squeal, a haunting sound,

He mourns 'em old tantalizing songs,
Soaked in a bottle . . . king cotton wine!

Charley gone, uh-huh, sleepwalkin' again

A tipsy mind at the crossroad lines,
A cunning Apollyon delivered a pact signed,
A wondering spirit, bouncing back and fro,
Dear God, rescue this poor immortal soul!

Papa, Charley gone, Charley gone
Sleepwalkin' again! Chasing 'em old bad dreams!

Chasing 'em old bad things!
He groans 'em old melancholy lies,
Held imprisoned by a plucking psaltery inside!

Dare to wake him, we tried! Shadow boxing
With Clootie, he cried! Mama, Charley gone,

Charley gone sleepwalkin' again!

Sir Charles

Underwater

Strength
From barbells
And leg lifts
Could never prepare
Your skin
To hold yourself
Together
When the world around you
Is falling apart
Wiping your tears
Like hands
In an ocean
I drown
To the very bottom
Swimming to the top
Is a joke I told myself
So I guess
I will learn
To breathe underwater

David Armenta

Thomas Wolfe in Our Memories

The train's whistle gleaming through mountains
pervades our essence
with a scintillating sound
The sunset is heaven's glow
We are wonderless
Nature has surprised our essence
We are all glowing with a
radiance of the setting sun
Tom would have been amazed;
the same sight and sounds as 1938
Was this the 2002 of the new Asheville
in Tom's "Look Homeward, Angel"?
We can see him smile at the
spirit of a mountain town
which grew in a boom
His mother's words could reverberate,
"Real estate is the soul of life"
God bless you, Thomas Wolfe

Alan L. Robinson

Hospice

I hold
Her withered hand
I listen to
Her yesterdays
Spaced
By tired breathing
And silent memories
I hear her sigh
See her smile
I know
She's home

William Devenney

Should I Remember?

Should I write another memory
About a lanky boy in khaki drab
Who, twisting his GI cap,
Shifted blistered feet
In boots too new
While standing there beside tracks
That shone and curved far out of sight
To a place called No-Man's Land?
And should I think again
Of that long wait and his face too white,
While I, with hair too tightly caught
By ribbons into a wartime snood,
Twisted a handkerchief of dampened anxiety
And remembered him instead in navy blue
With snowflakes frozen in his clothes;
A boy who stepped over the threshold
Into the holiday warmth of my home
And heart of love to leave his future there in my care
To reclaim it as a man shattered by a war
He wanted only to forget?

Dorothy Meyers

Walls

It wasn't until I met you that
I realized blue meant cold:
the blue of taps and walls
and eyes,
and not the blue of skies;
the blue of your veins
pulsing under Pygmalion skin,
your face a white marble statue
waiting for his gods
to let him in
because you have no say in
the matter.
You waited in ice ages,
round and smooth and cold;
he was trapped within shape,
yet you waited
and grew old.

Christina Curtis

The New Village
Circa 1920

I checked my gait and set my eyes to gaze
Upon the village tenements that stood
Aligned with others of its kind; in praise
Of former days, I'd trade for if I could.
They housed the folks who came across the sea,
Each thriving in their own peculiar way
To do what others did to make them free.
With names like Letourneau, Mikulsky, and McCrea,
Devries, Naroian, Maeringolo, Scott,
Extending graciously their talking hands,
And sharing with each other what they brought
In heart and holdings from their native lands.
As countrymen no need to stand aloof,
The tenements conceived a common roof.

Russell Bailey

How a Poem Writes Me

I firmly grasp my plastic pen
And wave it through the dark'ning air,
As language bids me greet the night.
Then 'cross the page the poem scrawls

Onto evening's balmy wings. Then
Words herd me to their hidden lair
Beyond the realm of human sight,
And language (songs of love) now lulls.

Above the grinding, earthly ken
Images and feelings rare
Parade themselves in spritely might
To illuminate my soul's spare walls.

Virginia Fry

The Stuff of Ghosts

Rags of fog levitate on dusky fields.
The ether swills. It threads and retreats,
swirls and snakes in liquid air. Eddies
wrap bundled hay protruding in the midst,
baled and bared.

Tight-wired bales rise from Earth's maw,
field teeth to chew at casual creatures
passing oblivious in the gnawing dark.
This is the essence of things obscured,
the stuff of ghosts.

The moist, lowering pasture is empty.
Timely, cows made collective way to the barn,
were milked, fed, sheltered for the night.
Roaming the river road, new spirits define
and reform landscape.

Here, damp breaths chill temperate sod,
lick trees' hems knotted in a hardwood clump
that centers these fields of creeping deep,
shroud trees' cronish knees, wrap skirts
around and around.

Helen Streeter Kelly

Color: The Gift Sublime

Of all our God's entrancing gifts, His most
Sublime may be the colors He devised
To flood the Earth with beauty that surprised
His childlike beings dwelling coast to coast.

Drawing light from His seven shining seas,
He sent it in lancets through stones called gems.
Through jade and emerald, if hues were hymns,
Green would have sung angelic rhapsodies.

White light through rubies brought a flaming glow
That gives the sunset its fantastic hue.
Sapphires suffused the sky to indigo
Above lawns holding petals small and blue.

Dissolving topaz into purest gold,
God sent forsythia to warm the world.
And far beneath the firmament's azure dome
His dandelions, glowing, graced each home.

What recompense, in fairness, did He give the blind?
A deepened insight? A creative mind?

Lord of our spinning world of stress and strife,
Your jeweled colors hallow human life.

Anna Margaret O'Sullivan

Standing Alone

Mother died in July; I was hot and sweaty
When I found out, I thought of the dark room she locked us in
Hiding her children like liquor
My grandmother looked like a nun
Smiled like she was the dead one
When they told me mother died
I wasn't at all surprised
She was always unreliable
That's the way I explained it the first time
And I wouldn't give up the idea
Even now when I tell this story
My mind is spying on my grief
As if it were my only visible image
Standing alone, out of control and forgiveness.

Shelby A. S. Waldecker

Artist's Profile
Jesse Castaldi
Somerville, MA, USA

"Aquifer" was inspired by the harsh cold of winter in Massachusetts, and by my own contemplation of the uneven brick sidewalks in Cambridge. The image of an unmapped reserve of water underneath the earth was very appealing, and the darkness of a frozen underground space mirrored my idea about New England winter. Winter is so often portrayed as a season of hibernation and stasis, but I see a lot of movement and destructive change there, and I hope "Aquifer" conveys that concept to the reader.

Aquifer

Here it is, winter, and familiar sidewalks
are unfamiliar, are puckered with cold,
buckling and tripping up your boot heels.
This ice that possesses concrete
has seeped up from the aquifer, they say,
through soil, through clay,
through unmapped bedrock.

Swim down, swim into it, half-frozen
and blind in the dark. Here you will find it,
the armies of water that amass in their subterranean caves,
that follow unseen veins up to the sidewalks
and push up the bricks with the frost.
They say there is water underground, they say this
but you want to see it: the roots of buried ice
that clutch winter roads and crack them
as easily as ice shatters the brittle,
enfolded tree limbs. Winter does not sleep.
You have seen it, how water breaks earth,
reaps breakage from the earth, an unseen insurgence,
a blind thing made wild, made king.

Jesse Castaldi

Empty Lullabies

Down long, sterile corridors
I followed silence . . . stony, cold
To automatic sliding doors
That expelled me into the black void
Of a night gone as lifeless
As the small, frail form
Lying somewhere beyond my reach
In the hospital's chill, foreign halls
The featherlike weight of the clothes he wore
Just hours before
When there was feeling
And warmth . . . and hope
Mocks the crushing emptiness of the void
That is my soul
I go home to piles of clothes
You'll never wear
And hum empty lullabies
While pieces of my shattered soul slide
As soft as you
Across my heart

Betty Sue Taylor

A Coat for Every Season

Spring wears a wispy, pale coat of green
To brighten the new season's day
Often she wears a delicate pink
Lavender, or soft peach, she'll display

In summer she wears a deep lush green
Bright yellow, vivid red, coast to coast
Her brilliant colors are so intense
She has every right to boast

Fall wears a blush of golden orange
Her burnished brown, a warm soft glow
Clear blue skies and very warm days
Still make our gardens grow

In winter she wears a glistening white coat
While snowflakes fall softly all day
A frozen world of icy beauty
Until springtime melts it all away

Doris Jean Miracle

in the framework of water lilies

swinging on their hinges, green porch doors
balancing, the last breath of day
letting in the sunlight through the cracks
in the floor, there were past premonitions
flickering here
my bare feet walking across lost corners
of thought . . . we are all huddled here
two long walks alone,
the candy coating scraped away to reveal
something alive without birth
the happiness
i am calling you underneath my covers
pulling up the sand in handfuls
with the salt and water mixing into one
(you find it smudged on your elbow)
the rawness of being an ocean away
from the street grocer who sells
bruised apples, you buy one listlessly
as i dream on the windowsill,
head resting gently down

Michele Catherine Lee

Plain Child

A plain child courted beauty
With the aching hope of a lover,
Trembling, about to discover
The blossoming grace of a lovely smile
Leaping to light in a small, wan face.

A plain child walked in beauty,
The echoing dream forgotten,
Walked with the still wonder
Of a new child begotten,
And knew not what they all saw
In the long, rapt hour—
That her wan face had the singleness
Of a sudden white flower.

Gwen Belson Taylor

The Forgotten Old Man

The old man sits so alone in the park
Browbeaten, unkempt, and tired from the dust
As the autumn leaves fall down all around him
The wind swirls up in a bone-chilling gust

His eyes are so faded, and the hope sadly gone
As he pulls up his collar roughly, he knows from hindsight
It will be yet another unforgettable cold and lonely fight
As he slides down on the hard bench for the night

He knows deep in his heart, as he drifts into sleep
Tomorrow will bring only much
Of the same heartache, he thinks
Despair, loneliness, and nothingness
As the tears start to seep
When he searches hopelessly, aimlessly
For his next crust and drinks

His fight for survival is a trait of today
Like so many homeless, he is forgotten and just swept away
With little means of support,
No shelter, compassion, or fight within
He sadly endures this cold, methodical
Society he now has to live in

Brenda Moran

The Migrant

As I stand here and look at the gum trees,
then up at the clear blue sky,
I wonder what can be missing, what's causing the mist in my eye.
I can see lots of hills in the distance,
but they're not the Mountains of Mourne,
yet still I should be so happy, but this isn't the place I was born.

I can see myself as a carefree child as I played in the purple heather.
It didn't matter not one bit about the cold, wet weather;
the spring was a time of magic then, the air filled with primrose scent.
Oh, dear, can those days be really gone,
can they really have got up and went?

The reflection I see in the mirror, can this really be me?
I can see an old white-haired lady where a redhead used to be.
The feet I did the jig with have now become so slow,
but I still feel very thankful they go where I want them to go.

I've still got all my memories, growing sweeter by the day,
and wherever I am in this vast world, they can't take these away.
So I'll sing of the wonders of Aussie, of the emu and kangaroo,
and I'll sing of the Mountains of Mourne
with their heather of purple and blue.

Lilian Adams

Artist's Profile
Reece Caterson
Carrum Downs, VIC, Australia

Reece was born in Sydney, Australia 1907 and educated at Sydney Girls High School; represented in New South Wales State hockey team. Reece became a physical culture teacher. Reece is a conservationist, painter, and potter. Warmed with three daughters Jan, Rosahnd, and Diana, and one son, James.

Bush Pool

It was the summer following we came
Back to the pool within the gully's fold,
Back to the clear green water and the bold out-thrust of rock.
The silken music across the cascade,
And we sat in sober joy beside its edge,
And ate and talked and smiled, just as of old.

Just, did I say? Not quite; a hollow sound
Echoed within our words as there I strove
To draw again that mantle of the past
About us, and re-hold the glittering things
That dazzled all my sight where first we sat
In rapture of the liberty we found.

The dazzling rock moved not, the pool lay dead,
The empty sand a barrenness of heat,
The trees stood rigid and aloofly calm
Before the craving of my questing feet.

And a great teardrop from the very heart
Gathered unshed behind the burning eye,
And the taut eardrum strained at every start
To catch again within the water's cry.

Reece Caterson

Artist's Profile
Fred Bendon
Allambie Hts, NSW, Australia

Born April 4, 1920 in London, England, one of thirteen children. In 1949, married Bertie Haggert of Boness, Scotland. Passed away 1972. I have one son, Stephen, married Noelene Barker of Sidney, Australia. They have three children, Kyne, Belinda and Dale, all grown up. My hobbies, math, playing keyboard and organ. Started to write poetry after a surviving three cancers: colon, bowel, and prostate. Given time to reflect and time to write, the result is inspiration. Poetry heals the wounds. I have had eight poem published by ILP and ISP.

There Comes a Time

Every child needs a lullaby
And one that they'll enjoy,
Whether it's a lovely girl,
Or just a sturdy boy.

There comes a time throughout the day
When you will have no choice,
The time they have been waiting for,
To hear your gentle voice.

They will stretch their slender arms,
And nod their little heads.
The time has come for all of them
To be set into their beds.

When another dawn awakens,
Into your room they'll creep,
Slide into bed beside you,
The end of a perfect sleep.

You arouse yourself as best you may,
You hear the hall clock chime,
The start of another glorious day,
When there always comes a time.

Fred Bendon

Lost

Hold me in your arms, Mum, as I lie down to die.
And please dry your tears, it's far too late to cry.
Do you remember the day I was born?
Was it late in the evening or the early morn?
And all of the things I was going to be,
What happened, Mum? What happened to me?
Why did I do drugs, I really don't know,
But once I started, my need it did grow.
Everyone did it, my friends and my peers;
Why didn't I know it would end up in tears?
I'm sorry, Mum, that you have to cry,
I always believed I was too young to die.
I feel like a bird, Mum, I feel so free,
How did I know, Mum, that it would kill me?
Now as I lie here, please hold me once more,
Then send me to Heaven where God keeps the score.

Georgia Arrigo

Street Santa

He has a plastic chair for his throne
With a thin cushion
For the scant comfort it brings;
His bell is perhaps a little tarnished,
His red suit may be a little tight,
He didn't seem to need all the padding this year . . .
His boots are hurting his feet again,
And his sack of goodies is a bit threadbare;
Even his beard is perhaps not quite as lush and curly
As some . . .
But at least it is his own . . .
And the children who climb onto his knee
To cuddle him tightly
And shyly whisper in his willing ear
See only his smiling eyes
And his loving heart. . . .

Helen Gosney

When Lightning Strikes

At a whim nature cracks fear with whip and might
snuffs out notable towers, twisting spires,
takes aim at trees and snaps a limb,
sparking bush fires, planting apocalypse in uneasy minds,
taunting howling dogs and haywire horses,
urging sharp, spiked, snorting bulls to fight,
rumbling, thundering, hooves pound and ignite.

From my attic I welcome the broadcast flash of light.
A static message crackles on talk-back radio
to batten down against boom and blast.
In the midst of the rage, I glimpse the greater sage in the sky.
With seeker's eye see a map of brilliant chalk tracks;
a skein caught on the blackboard of night—
new forks, new paths show un-thought of flight.

Frank Corso

Lunch Hour

Oasis. Cathedral square at noon
invites repose, its seats and sunlit corners
veiled in reverential silence.
The students come and go, the workers,
the lovers, rapt and lost to all the world.
A pause. Adagio. A spell's been cast,
and humanity's leveled by respite and repast.
A hand, omnipotent, has stayed its frantic pace
and each one sits replete, contented,
as if a miracle of loaves and fishes has been wrought
and the cathedral's storied windows come to life.
But Earth demands allegiance. Like brazen gulls
that pierce the silence and squabble over crumbs,
we must return to strife and toil. And we disperse,
the spell now broken, to worship at the shrines
of gods of clay, once more unwitting captives
until sunset and evensong call us home.

Asuncion Pritchett

The Twelfth-Century Moment

The two arrowheads lay embedded in your bleached bones.
The tiger's tooth you wore around
your neck lies beneath your skull.
A smile appears frozen in time.

Did the fire make you learn, was the shedding
of your skins and wings enough to let you stand?
Wind and thunder must have echoed your voice.
Lightning sharpened your high-held staff.

Twigs break, and the jays announce your arrival.
The bright moon you always walk by has yet to shine.
Leave your mark for me, so I may tell of your souls,
how we stood together centuries apart, expecting to meet.
Your spirit has slept and it drew our time ever closer.
At that moment, we use the same eyes to see.

You watched me wander into what is yours;
the trees masquerade your breath and the
silence conveys your position. And I spoke
to you once again. Forever I wait the
reply and halt my journey, not asking why.

Patrick Frost

First Encounter

There was first my father's hand,
stone strong and soft as April
on our blue-green Sunday strolls.
It gathered violets for me
in velvet leaves like hearts.
It lifted me into an August tree
to taste the sun in peaches.
On December—frosted windows
it found angels in white lace.
It showed me stars, "God's candles"
on our vesper walks to church
where incense rose like glorias
as he taught me how to pray.

Much later, I learned metaphysics,
read theology: Augustine, Newman, More,
sublime Aquinas with his proofs divine.
But it was not their winged words that gave me God.
I had met Him years before in my father's hand holding violets.

Marie Chiarella

Strings

I found an old guitar string
left abandoned in the grass.
Bent and forgotten forever,
crinkled nylon just won't last.

It served its purpose;
made music, then wore out.
Someone left it on the ground
for the wind to blow it about.

So I left this old guitar string
hidden in the grass.
It made me think of all the strings
I've left abandoned in the past.

Sue Rudd

Mariner's Psalm

Alone with the Milky Way
it's hard to believe in time.
Only the moment counts,
continues, infinity so vast
it's a womb to grow up in.
The sky, a canvas, moving,
constantly changing, night, day
always the same, but different,
our horizon past, present, beyond,
no walls limit such seclusion.
Eternity swings, anchored overhead,
our foundation in motion, restless,
serpentine beneath us, heaving,
rolling, a liquid filled with life.
Its depth an unfathomable chain,
having gazed out upon
the illusive periphery
where silver dances on water,
I have cried in the wind
and heard God's whispers.

J. Stephen Keller

Artist's Profile
Theodore Hewitt
Wolfeboro, NH, USA

The statue created by my mother's cousin, Vincent, is a masterpiece. My poem is a very brief account of a painful episode of World War II, one of many. All I have is a picture of the statue. I am flattered that my mother and I were the inspiration. Vincent also created "The Awakening" and "Eleanor Roosevelt." Soon after, I was in Europe in heavy combat (armored artillery). I was captured and escaped. Additional college at Biarritz American University. Was professional violinist, violist, and conductor. My writing abilities lean to prose (novels, short stories, etc.) My first submitted poem, "Goodbye," started my poetical interests. Colleges: Harvard, School of Education, Biarritz, France, American University, University of New Hampshire, Resaikoff Artist Studio. I'm old, but I still have a lively interest in the arts. Incidentally, I was among the first, if not the first, violinists on American TV.

The Embrace

Once, not so long ago, there was a world at war.
So many poignant farewells, a clinging together,
The dread of separation filled our lives.
Seared in my memory is Grand Central Station's big clock,
A timepiece for hello and goodbye.

Mother was late, my pass nearly over.
A stranger said, "Try the big clock on the upper level."
A dash to the escalator. She passes me going down.
Below, we embrace.
Cousin Vincent, sculptor, standing nearby, so deeply moved.
He creates "The Embrace."

How many people, how many tears,
How many missed meetings?
It no longer matters, except to those still here.
Ancient history develops so very fast.
Yesterday has gone forever.
Only a brief line of this history remains,
Unmindful of what once we held so important.

Theodore Hewitt

Stirred

Dying at ninety-two
on his hospital bed
in Grandma's old bedroom
next to his study
his firm voice at 3 a.m.
stirred me from sleep.

Foolishly, I tried to lift him.
We fell, unhurt, onto the carpet
where we stayed
until help arrived.

Later, "Will you stay until I sleep?"

"When I am gone, dearie, and they ask
what life has given,
tell them—everything.
Life has given everything!"
He smiled, drifting nearer death.
I cried into fuller life.

Julia R. Osborn

Time in the Snow

At the farmhouse in Cobden
When I make the bed I am
Only making the bed.
The dogs and I have the same sense of time
As the snow
And when we watch
It falling we are
Only watching the snow.
Napping on the couch under the
Picture window, the afternoon falls past effortlessly.
I wake now and then
To the sound of cows
Down the hill, through the woods.
At the grand piano,
When the sound of night can be
Just piano that's there,
There's a call
Of piccolo
Coyote voices
Only calling "coyote."

Jay B. Larson

Walking with an Unseen Grandchild

Take notice of this place, this now place
that speaks of joints swollen in protest,
of bones offering mantras against
the incessant pain of getting up
and getting on.
Count the many suns I have brought here,
you lithe and dew-touched child.
Let this place speak softly
of parched skin crinkling like once-green
palm leaves beside Sahara rivers.
See this ground where the horizon is clean,
where soil smells fertile and unknown.
I have come here leaping across chasms
filled with unmet challenges.
I have landed safely, clutching armfuls
of blank road signs for you to paint,
should you choose to come this way too.

Gloria Bush

Getting Across

This bridge by Monet
required no engineers.
Stress, resonance, materials
moot considerations
next to the artist's eye,
and what matter
with the safety net of waterlilies?
Impressionist bridges
don't have to be perfect.
All they have to do is reach.
Pity there aren't more,
even without the shadowing
and the vibrant colors.
Just the trajectory
of the determined arc,
reunited here and there,
embracing the deep echo
of sound arrived.

Nora Lane LaTeef

Self-Portrait in Thirty Seconds

I look at her with a half smile,
swiftly, making a quick assessment:

Admiration

The tilt of her head, only slightly upward,
marks a perfect blend of humility and pride.

Her form, indicative of a Southern heritage,
(and her civil attempt to control it),
is detailed by a smart suit in natural shades
that complements the rebellious black curls
that snuggle around her ears and
lap at the cappuccino coolness of her neck.

I smile again . . . widely, admirably,
as I meet her earthen eyes—
bright, focused, steely
in their concentration of my silent interrogation.
"You got a problem?" they ask:
Eyebrows arched dramatically,
lips pursed for an instant response.

I frown, avert my eyes quickly,
and turn away from the mirror.

Loris Nadene Adams

Idaho Blooming

The morning heaves upward,
Like the waking of the seventeen-year cicadas,
Across the plains' scabbed, flat-bellied girth,
A slow, subterranean cadence
That burns across this sad swath of dry countryside.

Through the back seat window of a white Volvo wagon,
I see Idaho bloom, a small town engulfed.
The skies ashen and sober, the faces of tea-stained paper dolls . . .
Not dolls at all but muddied, watercolor children,
Barefoot in the dirt.

On the cusp of an opium languishing summer,
Our car tongues the fire though a crumbled, linoleum town
And sears the crescent of road over the land's ochre geometry.
Then Idaho spills over with indolent determination,
A soft pursuit in dawn's buzzing distance.

Sarah Marie Panovec

Remembering Time

He was a small man,
wore tattered slippers,
and was content smoking pipes
from the rack

on the old radio.
His wife was delicate,
one could tell by
the embroidered cloth

on a wooden table and
her towels folded neatly
over the kitchen sink bar.
Threadbare rugs over time

And hard winters
made weather-beaten shingles.
But the peace in the meadow
and time went on.

ahe now-empty house
left an old, cracked cement porch
and broken mirrors like pools
of rain water. . . .
What of their children?

Jacolyn F. Roskowski

Wild Strawberries

Those delicious wild strawberries
I picked in my youth
As the locomotives passed by
Belching smoke, filled with cinders,
That is where the wild strawberries
Grew the best.
After the afternoon through freight went by,
I'd go to the side of the tracks
And pick enough strawberries
For strawberry shortcake for the evening meal.
With cream and sugar,
Now that was real eating.
Oh, for those little ripe, sweet morsels
That made my day.

Mary M. Stumreiter

Prelude to Abduction

How could you not have seen beyond that goblet
more poisoned with intrigue than any foreign court
and through that fire that so mysteriously sprang to life
in your unsuspecting darkened hearth
while you slept before it
your mind and napkin folded neatly back in place?

While they draped you in patriot's colors
and shot you full of infrared accusations
they ran rampant through a gentlewoman's sleeping brain
and left a thousand swirling jagged dreams to grow
then crept beneath her lowered lids
and plucked the sleeping flowers from her eyes.

Does that seem so strange to you
who had both seeds and shears
and valor of the kind
that saves the minds of men?

Amy L. Ventura

Nights in India

In those days
the night was left alone
to live itself undisturbed
by impudent city lights.
Dark was dark;
even light seemed to flinch.
In moonlit nights,
tall pines in distance
brooding priests and nuns
conviction perfect, immovable
in dark robes.
Nearer, champak and jasmine
breezed through the air
like love in vogue metaphor,
veined pebbles in memory's river
fond, unobtrusive art
rounded into peaceful calm
on forgotten shores.

Peace so calm
the enlightened Buddha could envy.

Anwer Beg

Rolling by Land

The highways across the great plains of Utah
connect the islands of civilization.
We dare not step out onto the arid plain;
we cannot confront the vastness of the distance.
Instead, we tread the familiar, ever touching
plastic, steel, cloth, and concrete,
benefitting from men and women who,
combined, bring us the
food, the chair, the roof, the toilet,
and the toilet paper.
But fellow travelers gaze
from innumerable vehicles,
taking gasps
of the freedom of open spaces
from the safety of the highway,
looking into the distance at the formations
of rock and earth and flora
under the limitless sky.

Becky Mate

Eternal Sleep

I'd like to store sleep
the way I store fat;
on my hips,
inner thighs,
the middle of my back
where the lace of the bra digs in.
When my reserves
overflow,
I could barter with others,
trading my sleep
for food or love,
blue eyes on Wednesdays,
theater tickets every other Saturday.
If ever
my storage places empty,
I'd ask God
to trade with me against
my cache of eternal sleep.
What would He ask for?
What could I give?

Mirela N. Trofin

The Pilgrim

A young man climbed the mountain
This morning to Assisi town,
A bedroll and pack upon his back
And garbed in a habit of brown.
Not one word passed between us,
But I saw on his cherubic face
The exhilaration he was feeling
Arriving at this glorious place.
I know not whence he came
And I know not where he will go,
But when he prays at the tomb of St Francis,
His young face will be all aglow.
Perhaps he comes to beg shelter
From his brothers, the friars in brown.
They'll feed his body and nourish his soul
Within the walls of Assisi town.
He arrived as I was leaving,
So I have an inkling of what is in store,
But to the backpacking Franciscan friar,
I'm sure 'twill mean even more.

Patricia Draper

Gypsy Child

Fragments of gaudy skirt
disguise dirty limbs
She stands boldly,
bare, dark-soled feet braced apart
to clasp in aching arms
her barely smaller brother
He sniffs on cue
thrusts a fist between dirty teeth
Head askance, she tugs at tourist sleeves,
squints through scattered curls
at the harsh, adult world
but passersby feign deafness
or ignorance of the currency
She shrugs her brother to the ground
Hands held tight, they run away

Margaret Eddershaw

Portrait of a Boy

A ragged, skinny, sun-browned country boy
With hat too big that was his father's pride
Whose solemn mien pretends his youth to hide
But from whose eyes the treacherous light of joy
Leaps out and ruins the little masquerade
See there upon the ground, a crooked pole
For waiting fish in dreaming water hole
Thus background has the truer picture made
A boy grows slowly in the mold of man
Those strange and sobering thoughts to which he bowed
Will pass like ripples on that magic stream
Where soon he'll lie upon the bright, hot sand
And whistle at a sky without a cloud
As spider-like, he spins his aerial dream

Evelyn A. Johnson

September Glory

In September a tinge of Indian summer
Settles down in Wisconsin's Door County,
Coloring leaves ochre, deep red, and crimson.
I find bleached bones of tree branches
Lying on a sandy shore.
Sometimes a breeze has a cutting edge
That flattens, patterns grassy slopes.
Happiness is planting purple cornflowers,
At least one gloriosa daisy
To grow perennial seasons.
That is a simple reason.
When the sun finds the horizon,
I walk a moonlit path through woods
Where stars make wonder bright.
And I wish, I wish a wish
To stay might be heard tonight.

Dorothy Ferg

Detour Taken

It's midnight now.
I sit alone, no TV and no telephone
to mar the silence in my room,
but inner ear still hears the tune
we bayed beneath a full blown moon,
then dared to let it die too soon;
this was to be our "very own,"
wither has the music flown?

Dim crescent moon's light touch on wall
where changing shadows rise and fall
as scudding cloudlets intervene
and weave an ever varied scene;
shadowed portraits of days past
fleeting dreams that would not last
parading in this sad tableau,
where did all our love dreams go?

With tired eyes, with weary heart
each night I watch our story start;
I lived the tale, I know it well,
must heaven's pathway lead to hell?

Jack Bowen

Untitled

She said her name was Marsha
her hands dangling from her wrists like wet clay
as she sat on the steel horse in the playground backward

They said her name was Carol
and she laughed from the bottom of her stomach

Roger with the body of a man pushes Carol to the sky
and her laugh bounces off the trees in the park

Roger's face fits like the pieces of a puzzle
sewn together with care
locking in a mind that will always see itself as only four
and then will always be as now and as before

They leave the playground like a small tornado
whisking leaves, rocks, and twigs from the earth
They disappear inside the yellow school bus
waving ever wildly as they chug down the road

Ducks still float on a leaf-covered pond
brown bark remains on the trees
and the blue-gray river flows perfectly

But there's no sound
only a stillness, an emptiness left in the park.

Jennifer DeSalvo Cortner

Colors

I bought paint.
I painted black, brown, red, and white on my skin,
Colors God did not wrap me in
So I can understand what it is like to look like you
Oh, African, oh, Hispanic, oh, Indian, oh, Caucasian.
To understand! Come, do it with me. Paint yourself.
Who cares if you drop some, making a spot on the floor?
Let it be a souvenir of what you have learned.
People can wash off paint, but not what they were born with.
So why object?
As I was in the shower washing it off,
I looked down beyond my feet
And I saw something I thought I would never see.
The colors were together as one,
In harmony, in peace. But they ran
Down the drain. Where did they go?
Come back! Only you can bring them back.
Go live together as one,
In harmony, in peace, with everyone who has a foreign color,
And if you see someone who is black, let them be,
Fore you were once black, you remember
As you look at the spot on the floor,
A souvenir you mustn't ignore.

Melissa Yates

Dusk to Dawn

The amber moon rises slowly,
Casting a golden glow
On all things beneath.

Gradually, the color fades
To a harsh white
As the last remnants of color
leave the opposing horizon
And dim to a velvet oblivion.

The moon, so luminescent
It obliterates all
But the brightest of distant stars.

Steadily the ebony backdrop
Lightens, and the glowing moon
Pales as the spectrum of light
Builds to rival the darkness,
And blooms into the dawn.

Lea Mall

fear

when they ask me
where i have come from
i am afraid to tell them
that i am from
where trees grow wild,
flowers remain unnamed

where birds cackle
through the solitude of night
and as they nibble up the darkness,
the sun rises from behind the mist-clad hills
and . . . as the day passes,
quietly goes down the meandering river

where the wet, steamy smell of earth
washed by the rain impregnates time
i wonder if i would ever find
a place more sweet and sublime

i am afraid to show them the way
to a place . . . pristine and unknown,
a place i have been parted with
for all these years that i have grown

Hiranya Nath

The Grandfather Next Door

The faint scent of honeysuckle
mixed with Aqua-Velva,
lingering in the air,
wrapping around me in the warm breeze of day
like water washing over a rock in the sand.

The sky fading from warm oranges to somber grays,
then to a coal black speckled with soft whites.
Speckled with stars burning millions of miles away
like front porch lights left beaming
so that you could find your way home.

All this flooded my senses
as we sat in two white metal rocking chairs,
talking about nothing and everything.
What the words were didn't matter.
I coveted each one as a secret that was
just between the two of us.

That is how he is remembered.
Memories branded in my mind.
Scars of what is now lost.
And though it was not by blood,
he was the only grandfather I have ever known.

M. W. Burton

Fountain of Youth

Drops of rain slip through
the tips of cracked fingers
where age is lying stiff
awaiting eternal youth
to find her there.

Wind falls against wrinkled skin
pushing her to follow
the sound of nature's voice
to the darkened water's edge

where a body tortured
by years of sewing clothes
watches time escape
to paint youth on faded
waves of water.

Tara Swisher

Cold and Thirsty

Stir your tea, Laura. Let the sugar dissolve,
separate from itself and become some other thing than itself.
Let the cream swirl and disappear evenly
throughout the stained and tinted water.
Swirling, turning, spinning my mind with
thoughts of you getting on that plane to leave me
here with him. He kept me from our last times,
him and this hypnotizing swirls.
Stop your swirling, damn it.
I have to stir it up, cause it to stop.
But I can't bring myself to do it.
Because it looks so undisturbed and under control.
If I were to grasp the spoon and blend together the ingredients,
I may start crying and never be able to stop.

Laura Davis

Margaret's Hands
For Margaret Higgins

Chafed from Kirkman Soap and old wood clothespins,
framed my chin,
a portrait still in progress, an art original as sin.
Crimson bled through contours,
hollows begged to be filled in.
Margaret's hands held cool rags to my forehead,
stroked the damp hairs from my face,
pulled strands, like fine distinctions, through her fingers,
rearranged life's pattern, tied it back in place.
Her fingers, dry as corn husks, bandaged knees,
rubbed at pain, an error that she might erase,
a stain, that yielding to her scrubboard
would rinse clean in the sink, and leave no trace.
Margaret's hands were fists that beat back time,
a savage pulse, a wanton fear,
the thing we both pretended that she never knew,
hidden in a shoe box with photographs and letters,
waiting to be found, to grab their due.
Margaret's hand hung loosely from a catheter
in Lenox Hill, medication dripping through the line;
her veins still bulged with effort,
that ache she chose not to define.
Her fingers clenched and gave one last transfusion,
opening as their strength passed into mine.

Patricia Kelly

Glassy Silence

We could talk politics, of course,
but look, the sun falls in an oblique angle
over the volcanic island's black sand
and death wraps itself
into the multicolored dress
of the most beautiful girl
and the city trembles with horror
and the old man still walks around
with a photograph stapled to his chest
warning that the end is coming
and other beginnings for which
I have no more strength.
We could talk politics, but look
how the world looks from the upper floors
frozen in its glassy silence.
In the end God takes care of everything
and of all things that He granted us,
the most valuable is forgetfulness,
to find each morning the sun
at the same place.

Carmen Firan

Artist's Profile
Pearl Foy
Langsport, Someset, United Kingdom

The futility of aggression/war always disturbs me. Like a lottery, it can go on and on in ever-increasing circles, many becoming entangled or destroyed, caught up in something that seemed a "good idea at the time," but ending with dire consequences. Two wrongs never did make a right, and many innocent people suffer unnecessarily. I am moved to write poetry now, as I was when I was a child. It is my way of expressing deep feelings, of communicating with people whom I may never meet, and by reading their poems, I am given an insight into another's persona.

Lottery of War

Dismembered buildings,
Dangling artifacts,
Like washing on a broken line,

Left in the path of the wind
From yesterday's terrors.
Ghost-whispers to those
Blasted from life
Or camouflaged by debris.

What blackbirds flew low
And, in flying, destroyed
Dreams and lives in pools of red?

Frightened eyes
Saw the distant border
In splintering light
That the black dove
Said was his,

But some knew
Was forever theirs,
And theirs and theirs and theirs.

Pearl Foy

Artist's Profile
Irene Cornish
Highett, VIC, Australia

I have a zest for life and an awe of the simplest beauties that surround us all, from the opening of a flower to the birth of a child. For one day only, I was to be a grandmother; the next, it was gone. This loss engulfed me, so I wrote of the love that nearly was. My "Dear Child" was penned in sympathy for all the women who have to deal with such sorrow of losing her unborn child. I have written numerous poems of tributes, love, and life experiences.

Dear Child

Never will I see the colour of your hair
I'll never know if your eyes are blue or green
Never knowing if you are a girl or boy
Dear child
You were never there

Never will I feel your hand on my face
Nor will I ever hear your cry
I will never hold you in my warm embrace
Dear child
I don't understand why

You existed only in a fleeting glance
Not ready for this world you see?
Never did you stand a chance
Dear child
It was not meant to be

I know that you will try again
As it is not your time somehow
But you will never, ever know my pain
Dear child
Sleep soundly, for now

Irene Cornish

Artist's Profile
Mark Collins
Dalby, QLD, Australia

True love is something that some people take for granted and is something that if we find it, we should cherish it, for some of us may never find it. Everybody has felt rejection and a broken heart, but as I write, there are some out there that feel it more than others. If you read my poetry and can relate to it, then you know exactly what I mean, so I dedicate this to all the girls I have loved but received no love back.

Prom Night

White dresses flow like satin rivers,
a cummerbund rainbow across a black suit sky.
Hair and makeup done like movie stars,
couples parade like royalty.
Hand in hand, in love till the end.
You hoped tonight would be your fairy tale,
only to find you are no Cinderella.
Your Prince Charming did not come;
tears roll down your cheeks
that once were glowing with happiness
of a night filled with love and laughter.
Only the laughter came from somewhere else,
and the love was nowhere to be seen.

Mark Collins

Artist's Profile
Vera Sandoval
Pomona, CA, USA

My poetry will always be about a passion of mine. I love the ocean. I can be rejuvenated by the smells of the sea. The vision of waves smashing against the pillars, the sound of foghorns, or seagulls flying above will comfort me instantly. As a youth, many wonderful times were spent at Newport Beach. We swam the entire day or sat at the pier fishing. Many times we came home with only a couple of smelt, so Dad would stop at the local fish stand. Newport Beach mesmerized us. I still feel the sand on my feet.

Sunset at the Newport Fish Market

The Newport tide was frigid as a bony matron,
Pelting spit from her icy lips
Here the Santa Ana winds bristled
With the voracity of a rabid dog.
It could be heaven; it could be hell.

Methodically, he worked his blue-numb fingers
Flinging, discarding fish heads for the feral cats
The strays would be out later,
Nibbling under a pock-marked moon,
Emitting their distinctive smell.

Diligent, mackerel-stained fingers worked,
Tucking, rolling, folding, wrapping fish.
Handing the dismal package of smelt to the senora,
His eyes said it all, "No pescado today,"
At least her children would have fish chowder.
He knew her so well.

In the distance, the Santa Monica horizon
Blushed in shades of crimson
While the moon awaited the next batch of astronauts,
But this was October in Newport;
Here, tenacity dominated,
How he loved this hell.

Vera Sandoval

Inching

Moments like this flicker
Like a candle at the seashore.
We did not know how long it would last.

There they were: embraced,
Moving side to side
On the embankment
That overlooks the interstate.

The long grass tickled my mother's knees;
My father's cheek grew red.

They spoke in whispers
That the sweeping clouds enveloped
And stole away from us.

Their quiet moment
Disturbed only by the
Gaze of two small daughters
As we got closer.

We were inching,
Climbing higher up the hill
To get a better look.

Jessica Anthony

I Sat Down by the River and Cried

I sat down by the river and cried
For it had told me many, many lies.
My tears overflowed, and as I leaned down,
I saw my reflection.
My warm tears fell down, and into the cold depths of the water.

Once a monk sat here. Here on the riverbank,
He enjoyed the sun, the gentle breeze, and the everlasting
Sound of the river covering smooth rocks.
He soon saw a scorpion float by, bobbing down the river.
Being pure hearted, this monk pulled the creature out,
Only to be killed by its sting.

Too many days this river lent me an ear
As I told the tales of my heart.
Its reply was cold and full of deceit.
I too saw a scorpion pass by one day;
I let it drown.

I turned my back on the river,
But even so, it still flows
Like the wind softly swaying trees, like clouds
Crying at night, I do not regret it.

Emily M. Odell

Artist's Profile
Barbara Matson
Borrego Springs, CA, USA

There comes times in one's life when the very act of rounding a corner can become an epiphany. The unexpected jumps out; water walks down a waterfall, a sea breathes back, a waving, sparkling field of oats holds captive a thousand bright red poppies, and waves them at you from afar. Words well up, and a poem is started from the conjuring of memories and metaphors. Just when you think you've seen it all, the Earth uproariously laughs and takes you on another trip to a place inside and out you've never seen before.

Surprise of Poppies at Snowshill

We round the corner to find
blood red poppies
clustered, perched, and shouting
on sliver-thin stems,
hundreds percolating in massive fields of seedy grain.

Their flaming mantles harbor
hum of striped and fuzzy bee
while fat green seed pods
nod promise of tomorrow on arching stems.
Today's blossoms face and track the light
of rise-to-setting sun.

Hmm,
do I hear warm chatter as they pirouette
among a sea of bronzing oats?
Their swaying bodies on one happy, hairy stem
bloom transparent red and paper thin.

Blooms released from prisons of historic text
of battles fought on Flanders Field . . .
to childhood memories
of a veteran's outstretched hand,
reassigned from buttonhole
to pleasant memory of an English countryside.

Barbara Matson

Home

When I think of home with its cozy nooks
With its winding paths and its babbling brooks,
I think of loved ones with whom I share
And wile away the hours in an easy chair,
Of perhaps a window o'er-looking the west,
Where one can dream dreams when his heart's at rest.

Where loved ones love and understand
And ever reach forth with a helping hand.
And the porch on a quiet afternoon
Where needles work to a little tune.
A book or two, and a cup of tea,
Alone, perhaps, or with company
While sunbeams play at hide and seek
Through the honeysuckle vine that conceals the street.

A little spin o'er dale and hill
Past lonely farms and an old sawmill,
A lovely walk in the twilight dim
When purple shadows creep softly in,
And as the stars begin to peep,
A loving kiss and peaceful sleep.

Helen Stoney McDaniel

Isolated

I am handed a pink corsage of flowers.
Pink for family, Mommy explains as she pins it to my yellow silk.
Fans whir, lazily blowing hot breezes across a sea of many colors
swallowed up by a thick, black cloud.
My legs dangle off the hard wooden bench.
I flip through the pages of the Holy Book,
strange, beautiful characters blurring.
Preacher speaks, but words, only words
of a foreign tongue floating out to nothingness.
Silence . . . engulfing, alienating.
Grandpa is up there,
little trickles flowing down his wrinkly face.
Daddy is next to me . . . Daddy, who never cries,
has droplets snaking down his cheek.
Mommy is looking straight at preacher . . . serious, stern.
Emma is curled up, fast asleep
blissfully unaware of hot and cold.
Sweltering heat settles like fog.
On everyone's face, drops of sweat . . . or are they tears?
And I . . . I am not crying.
The pink flower droops, wilting under scorching sun.

Sonya Hsieh

My Eternal Struggle (Where I'm From)

I'm from fake personas
putting on the mask for the world to see smiles cover up pain
Laughter covers up hate
From pent-up anger waiting to explode
fists clenched waiting to be unleashed

I'm from years of suffering
voiceless doctors delivering false hopes
I'm from dead brothers
from a coffin full of pain
I'm from suppressed feelings and lost hopes

I'm from a glimpse of hope
laughter emanating from the soul
true happiness, bliss
from escaping the darkness for one day
only to be submerged the next

I'm from my eternal struggle

Matthew Armstrong

Defrosting Solitude

Unwrap me slowly,
like a long-desired package
Gently at first, but with growing intensity
peel away the glossy veneer and reveal me
Exposed and shivering,
you cover me like a blanket
Your sunny embrace insulates me
dissolving the cold and melting my sorrows
Your lips travel the length of my spine
leaving a trail of vigorous green
Where hollowed stumps held dominion
emeralds grow to the sky
Flowers bejewel the wasted land
cascading joyfully down the peaks and valleys
Our breaths mingle in the morning air
inhaling the sweet dew that diamonds the grass

Jennifer Elizabeth Polidoro

My Gift

As I sit alone within my shade of grey,
I watch the flaccid night drift into day.
As time counts forth, here I must stay,
For here is where I come undone.

Left for not, yet for the choice.
Left unbroken, yet without a voice.
Burdens upon my back are hoist.
Why can't you see I am but one?

As I stumble through these restless days,
Milky vision turns infatuated gaze.
I understood as a figure I appraised,
As the essence from within did lift.

Form-fit flesh and an aspiring scent,
And eyes from blue to green they went.
Every given portion well-spent,
But come and gone so soon and swift.

Mercy! Take me from my shade of grey
And let come forth the blessed day
And let willing time count itself away,
For I am but my own gift.

Marcelle Eldon Neil

Seasons of a Relationship

Spring,
Of rebirth and rejuvenation
Remarkably light and carefree
Happiness abounds, a new creation
Nature awakens, reviving fertility

Summer,
Lazily drifting by a stream of heat
Hot desire burns beneath the skin
Balmy rendezvous so discreet
Joyously overflowing from within

Fall,
The beginning of the end
At first, unassuming, then bitter
Down a chilly path we wend
A barely contained titter

Winter,
All is lost
Frigid is the heart
Aside I am tossed
When at last we part

Andrea Bainbridge Orta

Heaven's Symphony

I smell the sweet lingering of notes
As the piano's melodic whisper
Irritates my senses.

The internal drumbeat of my heart
Sets the stage for surrounding mountains.

The oceanic symbols
Crash across my soul
Leaving echoes of nature
On the salt-sequestered paddles.

I sing somber lullabies
With the acoustics from a dream
As the soft strokes of fingertips
Put the mind at ease.

The wistful lyrics that flutter by
Grant flight to grounded roses.

The awe-founded song
Trickle tears upon the pillow
Creating a wishing well of melody
As weightless as a cloud.

Mallory A. Ingram

Marionette Theater

Lifeless, they hang there:
The blind prophet Teiresias
And Cadmus,
Ivy-crested staves dangling from their arms,
Garlands circling their old-man brows;
Dionysus himself, in the guise of a mortal man,
Panther skin hanging from his sagging shoulder,
Fair hair surrounding his enigmatic face.
Young Pantheus, King of Thebes,
Who had opposed the god of wine and ecstasy,
Still wearing the woman's wig and linen shift
In which he had gone to meet his death;
And Agave, blood-spattered,
Who, even in repose,
Cannot loosen from her fingers
The tangled hair of her son's severed head.

Carol A. Talley

Desert

Quiet and harsh,
Unbroken in the sun
A single bloom on the saguaro.
A goldeneye and a catclaw,
A horsetail rush or an
Indian paintbrush,
Red river, river sedge
Claret cup cactus along the hedge
Rattlesnake and mule deer,
Short-horned lizard and wild bear,
Canyon wren and catfish,
Blue heron and finch
Prickly pear and pinon pine, tumbleweed and time
Silk tassel and nightshade,
White fir or wild grape,
Gila trout and gray fox,
Oak creek canyons and
Red, red rocks.

Linda M. Call

Joshua's Brush

Old wood, stiff bristles,
and speckled steel solidify as

young eyes examine each groove
seeing the brush anew.

Tiny fingers, wrapped around a pencil
awkwardly sketch lines.

A soft tongue hooks his cheek,
tasting his goal.

Every muscle tenses as he
emphatically places graphite.

An artist's tool laid out,
an artist's tool in hand,
an artist's tool in flux.

Cathryn Carreer

Go Back

To when schedules blended into continuous ignorance,
And deadlines didn't breathe fresh life
Unlock the door of ideas rusting from criticism.
Re-drink the pools of adolescent love
From the dried spots on your pillowcase.
Replant the rotten fruit of first love
From the seeds of a hopeful heart
Before lipstick's touch and razor's burn.
Undo the buttons of tight-fitted blouses.
Reverse the strut tangled in your feet.
Freed from the desire of freedom,
Escape from stubborn reality
To imagination's open arms
Through the first blanket fort.
Enjoy sweet mud pies and princess dreams
In a time without time.
Go back, before growing up took an eternity . . .
Because you have eternity to grow up.

Alana Kim Dong

Ethereal Longing

Sparkling gulfs of azure blush
trusting, hoping, wanting
They beseech me with passion
yet gaze on with innocence
Dewy flesh of summer scents
amazing, delicious, speechless
Inhaling, I taste you
innocuously beckoning
Smoldering lips of want
sinful, heavenly, pure
Tasting of sweet anonymity
they part and call me forth
Velvety murmurs of harmonic degree
melodic, haunting, mystical
Your subtle tones
they bid me to follow
My senses ablaze
enlightened, growing, illusory
Do I pursue the intangible
or forever exist in tormented wonder

Amber Jade Farner

Fifth Grade

Wet air sets on tight skin
Among this hiding innocence
Muddy footprints quickly lose shape
While broken twigs and crippled growth
Reveal the direction we've taken
Youthful chatter echoes through trees
Boys we love who will never know
Concepts on how eyeliner is adequately applied
Secrets attaching themselves to the damp leaves
Voices choked with anticipation
Small fingers interwoven
We chant to spirits of our own creation
Making memories
Our own tired minds will forget in years to come
Covered up by late nights
Regretful mornings
Somewhere underneath
Our hidden footprints
Back home among the silent trees
Refusing to be released

Jillian Rabe

Santa Fe to Scottsdale

Seven hours by car
Across I-40
From Albuquerque to Holbrook
The High Desert plateau stretches
Blue sky forever across
Mesas and petrified wood
Then into the mountains of Arizona
Through Heber, Payson
Plunging down into the real desert
Yuccas, prickly pear cactus
Giant saguaros guard these western walls
Into the crevasses of the crumbling rock
We ride
Homeward
Towards the palm trees
Past orange groves
Landing just
Beneath the camelback

Nicholas Vitale

Chill Kiss of Autumn Bluster

Green leaves sprouted rust that
dripped bough to bough, splashing
drops of red across each leaf yellow by
nature's accord
Chill kiss upon cheek and
nose with icy love, blush-hued and bitter,
the bluster gives
Across the azure, grey milk spilled
here in clumps, there in wisps
Feet journey where the head has willed
heels tapping against remorseless slabs,
toes brushing the sad bough, fallen
Tree-sails, thick green, bolstered by the
onrushing fancy of envious mountains
Hear them wail the sad lament for gangrenous
summer when all about, nature lives
White and gold—wind and woe and I, wild
hair dancing with the dewdrop wind
on concrete perch with inky pen
immersed in time rendered

Kristopher Hendrik Omps

Lost

Moonlit sky of darkness came
Clouded mind of vision tame
Image shrouded, focus bent
Into swirling daze was sent
Drifting, drifting, all around
Tripping, falling, without sound

What is found there may not seem
Concrete art of that we dream
Covered in a sense of glaze
That we do made into maze
Twisting, turning, in and out
Bobbing, weaving, without doubt

Freed the very captive soul
Made the body one as whole
Distance covered vast and wide
Nothing nowhere cannot hide
Looking, searching what was sought
Running, chasing after thought

Thomas Joseph Arters

Heat Wave

The hum of a solitary fan in a darkened room
Warm, stale air circulating with dust
Offering little relief
A dog pants, seeking out a cool cement floor
Outside, a contrast
The glare of a bright blue sky
Sun scorching new growth of seedlings in terra cotta pots
Footpaths blistering the skin of barefooted soles
Once-empty beaches
Crowded with red-skinned bodies in board shorts, bikinis
Sand flies stuck to zinc-covered noses under colorful hats
Ice creams ingrained with sand curdling around the cone's edge
Salty-tasting drink bottles, peeping from backpacks
Children making sand castles, wading where tide meets sand
Reveling in the froth of exhausted waves
Resembling toddlers in a bubble bath
Feeling the coolness of seawater
Obscuring the humidity of the heat wave

Janet Christine Robinson

Cheer Up, Sleepy Jean

On rainy days, we sang together,
sipping lemonade
and strumming the guitar,
completely oblivious
to life beyond the front porch
and drunk with happiness.

On moonlit nights, we lie together,
gazing at stars
and questioning faith,
consumed by emotions
of evolving love
and deepest fears.

But a summer crush
was not enough
to keep him with
a delicate girl.
So beneath a whisper,
he let me go,
while humming the refrain
to "Daydream Believer."

Megan Nicole Spain

The Knowing

Piece by piece,
you peel away
the calloused layers of emotion
which I have built up over the years.

Slowly, gently,
you remove the masks
which hide me from the world,
exposing me to the light,
forcing me to trust you.

One by one,
I drop the screens
I hold before my mind.
Until finally I stand before you
in naked truth,
and still you do not turn away.

This, then, is love.

Tommy Dewain Howe

Iniki

Stirring out at sea
Lightning thunder wind and rain
Fury of the gods

Daniel Kahapea

Sunday Semi-Morning

The old armchair
recovered in thick gray wool
I sit
Sunday morning
snubbing gravity
I slide down, my legs lifted up
fetally, as in bed
but now
in that old chair
positioned by my mother in a manner she thought artistic
near the front window
out of which I stare
without my glasses
without fore or background
allowing vague impressions of leaves to smother me to sleep

Perrin Kristina Drumm

Naive Me

Today I spied a grape
that never got to be . . .
it clung to the mother-vine
on the thickness of a thread.
Its pinhead green-being
suspended, almost nonexistent,
next to its purple-plump partners.

That minuscule grape
that never got to be
reminds myself of me . . .
this lack of sustainment
means stagnation,
yet agonizing longevity.

Because I was so naive
you never chose to consume me.
And I'm cast away to
rot . . . yet always remember thee.

Lisa Mikula

On the Muni in San Francisco

I remember the murals of the SS in the sub-basement
of the caserne in Nuremberg
you shoveling coal into the furnace that heated us all
Hemingway and Castro were your heroes
Jesus and Kennedy mine
You, Theo, and I would recite poetry
behind the lectern in the marble-rich chapel
discuss politics in front of a "National Geographic" world map
We wandered around the infamous wall
and filled our heads with futile fantasies unfulfilled
rendezvoused with our favorite Friday-night frauleins
and took leave to Amsterdam, Paris, and Rome
That was a simpler time
when we'd unearth Nazi artifacts and discover their bold
and embossed belt buckles with the outrageous insignia:
"Gott Mit Uns"
That was a simpler time for us
not quite comprehending the bellowing smoke
that shrouded Dachau
blinding the eyes of the bishop

Philip Hackett

Todd Performing under Coffee Tables

Hot breath bleeding into microphones
Tapping iron stools through retina embraces
Lipton tea bags fog . . . falling from mirrors
Low lights shadowing plastic cups that seep
Clover honey . . . lemon peels balance
Rows on fermenting plates
Lags around metal chairs
Holding liquid by its palms
Fading black jeans
Shoes . . . no socks . . . falling from eucalyptus toes
Swaying left and right
Echoing voices sift in dry
Camel cigarettes
Contemplating obscure endings
To Calvino and Bergman
Above ashtrays

Jessica David

Untitled

While sipping bamboo tea
soft voices whispered
as she-dragon cups found
geisha handles clicking
painted smiles into Mama's face
So begins the cosmic dance
a fragility of existence
Crystal slippers
tiptoe
waltzing across a clabbered sky
Percussion echoes
sweet virgin birth
throbbing, pulsating wildly
beckoning, teasing our
immortal jugular vein
Rituals crescendo in the
mist of sacredness
each mystic breath
an unborn symphony
unfolding . . .

Renie Burgess

Spider

Spider,
Why are you in the tub while I'm showering?
I'm not a Buddhist, you know.
And you are brown . . . you're not a deadly recluse,
Are you? If so, why aren't you hiding?
Maybe you just came out of that loose partition.
Here's a splash; why don't you scamper?
You are a shirttail relative of the scorpion,
And I always murder scorpions.
Splash; oh, you'd rather not go down the drain.
All right, climb on this rag,
And I'll throw you out on the floor.
There, I saved the bugger.

Does that mean I can avoid another incarnation?
No, I suppose that won't make up for all of those
Flies and mosquitoes whom I've offed.
Another incarnation might not be all bad;
This one has had its moments.

Knute Stiles

The Fire-Cherry

A large green candle in the field
she stands alone
and you can see
where nature's fury opened her
and almost snuffed her out
six years ago.
The yellow finches came to help her,
chose that wounded body for their home,
so she, entranced by all their shiny singing
refused to die
and with one ember of her own deep fire
began to grow herself a whole new trunk
believe it
from a single branch.

And you, what of your fire
and the golden singer in your soul?

Gabriele Mayes

the lilies made me cry

the lilies made me cry
but you weren't looking
i hid behind the woman
in the umbrella hat
i heard the riffles
twenty-one
echo off the church
forty-two
and the emptiness
in your mother's voice
i watched the children
play
not a care that god
was watching us all
as we laid our saint
to rest that day

John Joseph Zenk

"Arroz y Frijoles"

I had gone there to take pictures.
There she was,
the one I call my friend . . .
although I've slipped before,
in the dark pit of her eyes . . .
and never quite known.
But when she cooked,
my blood was renewed.
Meat crumbled beneath her fingers,
cilantro sprang
between the onion and tomato;
my soul could breathe again.
Standing in her kitchen,
our skin fragrant with "el arroz y los frijoles,"
I remembered how simple life once was.
I had gone there to take pictures.
How long have I been starving?
Feed me forever, blood sister!

Jerika Carmen Daleo